UNIQUE EATS AND EATERIES

OF

ST. LOUIS

Suzanne Corbett

Reedy Press
PO Box 5131
St. Louis, MO 63139
www.reedypress.com

Library of Congress Control Number: 2017934687
ISBN: 9781681061146

Printed in the United States of America
17 18 19 20 21   5 4 3 2

DEDICATION

In memory of Jim, my old woolly bear, who shared
my joy of food and savored everything he ate.

CONTENTS

GLOBAL GRUB

PLATES WITH A PAST

MARKETS AND FARM STANDS

SMOKED, CURED, AND SAUCED

HOT HEARTHS, COOL CREAMS

ST. LOUIS ITALIAN

YARD BIRD DINNERS

DINERS, DELIS, AND DRIVE-IN DIVES

INTRODUCTION

I must confess, I often find myself dreaming of dining destinations of days departed, such as the first Orient restaurant at 414 N Seventh Street across from the Ambassador Theatre. The old Orient offered 401 items on the menu, including my favorite, the oyster subgum chop suey with white mushrooms and English walnuts, sprinkled with white pepper and topped with sliced scallions.

It'd be oh, so good to go back to Garavelli's Buffet at 3606 Olive, a little east of the Empress Theatre, to sit in a balcony booth and be served by the white-jacketed waiter Andrew, and enjoy the best toasted ravioli prepared in a way not seen since, or the turkey and dressing . . . and so much more.

The tiny Toddle Houses, such as the one on Lindell next door to the Arthur J. Donnelly Funeral Parlor, served a chopped steak sandwich and icebox pie that were terrific treats, and they had the best hashbrowns of all, although Kopperman's on Franklin and then N Euclid came close. I can't leave out Beffa Brothers Buffet, with great beef stew on Tuesday, or Sala's Under The Viaduct on Daggett and S Kingshighway, where the Sala Special sandwich was our town's finest sandwich ever.

Somewhere in time, someone will likely be wistfully waxing about the eats and eateries as documented herein by Suzanne Corbett, our time's reincarnation of Duncan Hines. Her carefully concocted compendium of eats and eateries attests that she is the queen of cuisine in St. Louis, and you cannot go awry by following this gastronomy guide. Knife and fork in hand, I'll be right behind you.

—Ron "Johnny Rabbitt" Elz

Ron "Johnny Rabbitt" Elz
Rabbitt, now in his 63rd year in broadcasting,
hosts "Route 66" Saturday nights on CBS Radio
KMOX AM1120, on which he fills the airwaves
with music and memories of the 1950s and '60s.
A passionate St. Louis historian, Ron serves
on the board of the Mercantile Library & Art
Museum, the Field House Museum, and Screen
Actors Guild–The American Federation of Television & Radio.

FOREWORD

HUNGRY FOR ST. LOUIS

I'm hungry. Hungry for something different, something familiar, something savory, and something sweet—something found in and around St. Louis that satisfies what I uniquely crave. Those cravings have driven me to sift though mountains of menus, shop baskets of groceries, and explore countless eateries. Places where foodies flock and the culinarily curious gather. Places that I always return to hungry.

Perhaps you're hungry with the same cravings I have, maybe not. My cravings, like my unique picks, will no doubt wildly differ from what you crave or find exceptional. My picks may excite some, while others will deem them ho-hum, as interesting as Saturday night's leftover pizza. And that's okay. Because that's the nature of the culinary experience. You like what you like. It all depends on personal taste, ultimately resting on whether or not you enjoyed the eats and the experience.

That said, this book is a personal short list of places and foods that sing to me. Picks were tough because I could have included more. In choosing these picks, I decided to abandon the trendy, the here-today-gone-tomorrow fashionable haunts. Instead, I assembled culinary themes based on specialty, background, or history—allowing my affection for St. Louis classics to guide me. The result that follows is an eclectic mulligan stew of suggestions that are all over St. Louis's culinary landscape. Each is presented as a vignette that has been boiled down not unlike a sweet sugar glaze designed to stick in your brain, to retrieve the next time a craving strikes. A total of ninety-nine eats and eateries are each waiting to be discovered, or in many cases, rediscovered. These places fill St. Louis's smorgasbord with variety, promising to satisfy cravings and guaranteeing no one will leave St. Louis hungry.

GOOEY BUTTER AND BEYOND

It's impossible to talk St. Louis eats without paying homage to its iconic foods, starting with gooey butter cake and toasted ravioli. Both have disputed pasts with contradicting claims of where and who invented them, which I won't rehash here. However, I will confirm the facts: both culinary mishaps paid off big time. They both became true mid-century modern culinary wonders, thanks to our transient nature and the Food Network, which have taken gooey butter cakes and toasted ravs beyond the Gateway City.

Toasted ravs have popped up nationwide, even gaining consideration from McDonald's, which test-marketed them. Gooey butter cakes have surfaced on menus from Los Angeles to New York City. Paula Deen has even tried to lay claim to the gooey butter—baking it in several flavors for her Savannah, Georgia, restaurant, The Lady and Sons. Of course, nothing bests the originals. It doesn't matter how the ravioli is stuffed or how the gooey butter tastes because it's all good.

St. Louis's legendary eats extend miles beyond the venerable gooey butter. Most of those distinctive St. Louis dishes revolved around the favored food popularized by the everyday working class Joe and Jane, simple delicacies, craved for decades, that transcend generational preferences and are celebrated by foodies. These are standout eats, which in my opinion are unique eats with great stories and excellent flavors I'll always crave.

THE ST. PAUL SANDWICH

Egg foo young on white bread, dressed with lettuce, tomato, pickles, and mayo, a concoction whose lineage varies depending on who's relating the story. I credit its birth to Park Chop Suey, in Lafayette Square, where Steven Yuen assembled the St. Paul, christening it in honor of his hometown. Some say the St. Paul is related to the Denver Sandwich made by Chinese cooks who worked for the western railroad workers in the last two centuries. Perhaps, yet St. Louis has a firm grip on this sandwich and its hometown claim.

ST. LOUIS-STYLE THIN CRUST PIZZA

Pizza on a cracker. That's what St. Louis' thin-crust pizza has been called. It's been called a lot of other things, too, by non-St. Louisans who malign it from crust to the shredded Provel topping. So what drove thin crust? I feel it's economics. It's cheaper to make—thin crust bakes fast, isn't generally overloaded (densely stacked) with toppings, and features Provel, its signature cheese, created as a blend that was originally cheaper than mozzarella. The St. Louis thin crust must be square cut, as proclaimed by Ed Imo, a tile setter who cut his pizza like his tiles.

PORK STEAKS

Another brainchild that made a star out of a cheap, unwanted meat cut, the Boston butt or pork shoulder roast, attributed to the local butchers working for Schnucks Markets. Pork steaks became the center of the backyard grill, and they were grilled fast, then soaked in sauce. Pork steaks are the reason to this day that St. Louis uses more barbecue sauce than any other city in the country.

ST. LOUIS SLINGER

Stack as follows: fried eggs, hash browns, hamburger patties or a cheap, thin-cut steak; cover in chili with or without beans; then top with cheese and onions. Ta-da! The St. Louis Slinger, the preferred food of the late-night crowd, namely college students and the overserved. O.T. Hodge Chili Parlors and Big Ed's Chili Mac's have dished the Slinger for nearly a century using the same chili recipe made famous at the 1904 St. Louis World's Fair.

COBBLESTONE BREAD

Truly one of St. Louis's most distinctive food items, one which is often overlooked. Cobblestone bread uses a cream-style/white bread dough that's torn into pieces, placed in a square loaf pan, and drizzled with egg wash, which seeps into the loaf as it rises and bakes. Once baked, it gets its "cobblestone" top. St. Louis cobblestone bread is a rarity found at small, old-time bakeries, such as Lubeley's or Federhofer's.

THE GERBER SANDWICH

Italian-style bread, spilt in half, spread with garlic butter, topped with ham and Provel cheese, sprinkled with paprika, and toasted. That's the Gerber, the open-face toasted sandwich that may well have inspired today's toasted sammie craze. Created by Ruma's Deli in the 1970s, it was named in honor of a loyal customer, Dick Gerber.

DAD'S COOKIES

Dad's Original Scotch Oatmeal Cookies seem like a St. Louis original, but they're not. In truth, they were part of a popular 1920s franchise. St. Louis is the last outlet, still operating at the same bakery shop location since 1938. Still weighed on an old-fashioned scale and packed in brown bags tied with string, they're a classic best enjoyed with ice cream.

TED DREWES FROZEN CUSTARD

Forget the cones, sundaes, shakes, and malts. I'm here for the concretes, from the place that claims their invention. The concretes are a specialty that cemented the shop's reputation and helped elevate Ted Drewes Frozen Custard to landmark status along Missouri's old Route 66.

HOME TOWN CHIPS: OLD VIENNA RED HOT RIPLETS AND BILLY GOAT CHIPS

The yin and yang of St. Louis potato chips—polar opposites, one old-school commercially produced, the other, artisan handmade. Red Hot Riplets are the signature chip that revived the Old Vienna brand for its fans. Billy Goat, the chef-inspired kettle-cooked chip, is craved by foodies and anyone who enjoys a robust chip that doesn't lose its flavor under the dip.

MAVRAKOS AND BUSY BEE CANDIES, ST. LOUIS'S RESURRECTED CANDY BRANDS:

We have affection for confections, especially for St. Louis's most famous historic candy companies, whose recipes and traditions could have been lost if Chocolate Chocolate Chocolate Company had not resurrected the historic recipes and brands. Fans of Mavrakos Pecan Burrs and chocolate-covered Molasses Puffs have celebrated since their return. Busy Bee Chocolate, founded in the 1880s by the Candy Brothers (no joke) and closed in 1959 to the dismay of St. Louis's chocolate lovers, is back. A historic assortment box of chocolates is based on Busy Bee candies, recreated as a fundraiser for the benefit of the Campbell House Museum.

UNIQUE EATS AND EATERIES

OF

ST. LOUIS

PLATES WITH VIEWS AND GARDENS

INDIA PALACE

Lovers of airplanes and authentic Indian food will be thrilled. Location and view: the 11th floor of an old Howard Johnson hotel overlooking St. Louis Lambert International Airport's runways.

11380 Natural Bridge Rd., Bridgeton
indiapalaceairport.com
Photo credit: India Palace

CIELO'S SKY TERRACE AT THE FOUR SEASONS HOTEL ST. LOUIS

Sunny blue and starlit skies could be considered Cielo's off-the-menu specials. And why not? "Cielo" translated from Italian means "sky." Even its location is lofty, on the eighth floor at the Four Seasons Hotel St. Louis, located along the northern edge of Laclede's Landing. The main dining room boasts floor-to-ceiling windows, which open onto the Sky Terrace, where guests can sip craft cocktails while drinking in expansive unobstructed views of the newly landscaped and designed Arch grounds.

Beyond the view, Cielo's Sky Terrace landscaping and a reflecting pool provide a rooftop oasis within the St. Louis urban downtown desert. This place encourages one to linger over plates created by Italian-born chefs, all vetted and brought to the Four Seasons Hotel St. Louis to develop its menu based on classic Italian culinary techniques and locally sourced products. The results have yielded inspired dishes designed to delight guests, from the hotel's traveling hipsters to local foodies.

Photo credit: Four Seasons Hotel St. Louis

The Sky Terrace's standout is the private cabana dining, a must for romantics or those simply wishing to be alone—another option the hungry and thirsty can enjoy while taking in the river view or late-night stargazing. The only thing that may rival the view will be the chef's plates.

999 N Second St., St. Louis
314-881-5800
fourseasons.com/stlouis

CAFÉ OSAGE

Secluded gardens have always sprouted interest, especially for those fond of dining al fresco. Café Osage possesses such a garden, which sprang from its sister operation, Bowood Farms, a nursery/garden shop that opened in 2006 in the Central West End neighborhood.

Café Osage is located along a less-traveled strip of Olive Street that some would consider off the beaten garden path. Keep an eye peeled—it's easily overlooked. The garden is hidden behind a wall and gate—a seasonal hot spot for business breakfasts and ladies who lunch. An overflow from the garden shop and the main dining room, the garden courtyard serves as a place to peruse the plants before ordering lunch.

Dining inside or out, patrons can expect a menu featuring uncomplicated soups, salads, sandwiches, and breakfast plates based on organic ingredients. A menu standout that Dr. Seuss would applaud is the Greens, Eggs, and Ham. Other picks worth mentioning are the Brie L T Sandwich, spread with tomato marmalade, and the citrus salad, a gourmet's delight that mixes arugula, fresh mint, red onion, almonds, and goat cheese with a lemon vinaigrette.

Garden seating fills fast during the temperate months. Even when the weather is dicey and raindrops fall, some guests don't mind huddling under table umbrellas for the opportunity to sip and savor in this urban garden.

4605 Olive St., St. Louis
314-454-6868
bowoodfarms.com

Photo credit: (top right) Bowood Farms; (left, middle right, bottom right) Suzanne Corbett

PANORAMA

The St. Louis Art Museum in Forest Park didn't have to give a lot of thought to the name it chose for its restaurant, Panorama. Panorama is exactly what you get, a panoramic view afforded by the floor-to-ceiling windows that run the length of the dining room. The view frames the lawn and stands of trees near Shakespeare's Glen and was no doubt a consideration for David Chipperfield, the renowned British architect who designed the museum's East Building. The building is the most recent major addition to the museum, whose original complex dates to the St. Louis World's Fair in 1904.

It's a pleasant view to feast on before your plate arrives, and most seats face it unless you're seated with your back to the window. In that case, twist in your chair and check out the view, and then check out the menu—you'll find a seasonal connection that mirrors the changing colors of the trees. Those changes drive the kitchen to focus on seasonal, locally sourced products. So expect real spring greens served in spring and hearty winter vegetable soups served in colder months. There are a few non-seasonal menu mainstays, such as Panorama's fresh-dressed Caesar salads and burgers topped with artisan cheese. Of course, all items are artfully prepared and plated to delight the senses, just like the art collections that fill the museum.

1 Fine Arts Dr., Forest Park
314-721-0072
slam.org/dining

Photo credit: (left) Suzanne Corbett; (right, both) St. Louis Art Museum

Special exhibits often inspire Panorama's Executive Chef Ivy Magruder to create special plates or dining events. Check the website for menu features and special events and don't forget diners get a discount on garage parking. Bring your dining receipt to the information desk for validation.

KEMOLL'S

Trace the locations where Kemoll's restaurants have operated over the last ninety years, and you'll find this family-owned institution has been on an upward track. When Kemoll's first opened in 1927, it was a one-room, ground-level confectionary on the city's north side. Its current location is perched on the fortieth floor of One Metropolitan Square, a location sporting commanding views of the city, riverfront, and Illinois landscape.

While window tables are prized for their views throughout Kemoll's multiple dining rooms, the rest of the tables aren't shabby either. Kemoll's vintage décor, a holdover from the late Noonday Club, is a throwback to a more elegant time—when a sky view paired with fine dining was an indulgence. It still is. Classic views enhance the dining experience, delivering a touch of old-school savoir faire. From a menu replete with Kemoll's gourmet family recipes, be sure to experience the Filet Douglas, sauced with Cognac cream and crowned with lobster, and the garlic cheese bread—both mainstays on the menu years before there was a view to enjoy.

To guarantee the best view, make a reservation requesting a window table. Without a reservation, you'll have to take your chances on window availability. But don't worry, window table or not, when you're on the fortieth floor, the view served with your plate is great.

1 Metropolitan Square
211 N Broadway, St. Louis
314-421-0555
kemolls.com

Photo credit: Kemoll's

BIXBY'S

St. Louis's various cultural institutions provide some of the best dining views. Bixby's, housed in the Missouri History Museum, is one such venue. Bixby's made history by being named as one of the Food Network's Top Museum Restaurants—a list that numbers only seventeen establishments nationwide. It was the only Missouri museum eatery that was honored by the Food Network, which applauded Bixby's inspired, stylized cuisine, relaxed atmosphere, and view. That view was created by the contemporary window curtain wall that hugs the length of the dining room, providing expansive park views easily enjoyed from any table.

Located on the museum's second floor, Bixby's is a full-service dining experience and is complemented by its sister operation, Bixby's Express, a grab-and-go food bar tucked into an adjunct alcove. Bixby's Express's fast-casual chow-down option provides tables that spill out onto the second-floor balcony overlooking the museum's atrium. Granted, it's not the park view that the main dining room offers, but it's a view nonetheless that's a great place to perch, nosh, and people watch.

Bixby's is a popular lunch destination, so expect a wait if you don't have a reservation or arrive during the lunch rush. To ensure a table along window row, call ahead and make a reservation or reserve online, where the latest seasonal menu is posted along with special themed dining events based on the museum's current exhibits.

Missouri History Museum
5700 Lindell Blvd., St. Louis
bixbys-mohistory.com

Photo credit: Bixby's

THREE SIXTY

The name says it all. For the price of a drink and the occasional cover charge, one can sip and savor downtown views from east to west, north to south. Three Sixty, one of St. Louis's largest rooftop patios, is housed in the Hilton St. Louis at the Ballpark. Hovering 400 feet above street level, Three Sixty provides a bird's-eye view 365 days a year. The bar's view attracts the local crowd along with the tourist trade, who come to take in the sights of the Gateway Arch, the riverfront, and Busch Stadium, especially during Cardinals home games. The rooftop draws Cardinal Nation's faithful fans, as well as the baseball curious, who don't mind the standing-room-only crowds peering into the stadium and following the action on flat-screen TVs.

Whether there's a game or not, outdoor and indoor bars keep thirsty customers and fans satisfied with a roster of wines, local beers, and craft cocktails, including signature cocktails that change with the seasons. When hunger strikes, Three Sixty dishes up an impressive roster of full-plate options, such as hanger steak and salmon. Not so hungry? Then graze on small plates and appetizers, which are easier to juggle when jockeying for prime viewing positions on game day.

Hilton St. Louis at the Ballpark
1 S Broadway, St. Louis
314-241-8439
360-stl.com

Photo credit: Three Sixty

Consider visiting the rooftop beyond baseball season.
Three Sixty's rooftop is open throughout the year, making
it a cool destination during the colder winter months when
the sky is clear and the fire pits glow.

One might wonder why Forest Park has so many unique eateries. I can answer that in four words—great views and history. Forest Park, established in 1876, served as a centerpiece for the 1904 St. Louis World's Fair, which featured an elegant lagoon system that meandered through the park. The Boathouse is built on those remaining waterways, now dubbed Post-Dispatch Lake, where rental boats can ply the waters with a bevy of resident ducks while customers dine lakeside. The Boathouse is a charming location for anyone trolling for waterside al fresco dining, and the tables are among the most sought after in the park, making it a popular pick that's open year-round for lunch or dinner.

The menu may have been influenced by its lakeside location, considering its impressive seafood selection, which includes cod, shrimp, salmon, and lobster in such dishes as Guinness-battered cod, lobster nachos with chipotle aioli, and seafood pot pie. Carnivores won't be left waiting on the Boathouse dock. Chicken, barbecued pulled pork, and burgers round out the menu overseen by Catering St. Louis.

When dining dockside, don't forget to make arrangements for the lake's feathered beggars. The ducks will vie for a free meal in exchange for their dockside entertainment.

6101 Government Dr., St. Louis
314-367-2224
boathouseforestpark.com

Photo credit: Boathouse

When The Muny is in season or when Forest Park is hosting special events as the V.P. Fair or Balloon Race, make reservations or expect long waits. Otherwise take a boat ride to pass the time until your table is ready.

CAFÉ MADELEINE AT THE PIPER PALM HOUSE

Back in the late 1800s, fashionable St. Louisans took Sunday strolls through Tower Grove Park and marveled at the South Palm House greenhouse. After almost 150 years, guests can still come stroll the grounds and brunch amidst the greenery inside the Palm House, now the Piper Palm House, home to Café Madeleine.

Café Madeleine, operated by Butler's Pantry, has become St. Louis's ultimate Sunday brunch. Among the Victorian greenhouse's palms, ferns, and potted plants, guests feast from three overflowing buffet tables, each artistically displayed and filled with an upscale assortment of hot and cold foods along with a special station designated for custom-baked desserts. On the menu are seasonal chicken, beef, and pasta entrees along with classic breakfast fare, salads, fresh fruit, and smoked salmon. Decadently rich pastries, muffins, bread puddings, and of course, madeleine cookies rule the dessert table.

Café Madeleine's menu and the Palm House's interior foliage are seasonally tweaked. Beyond the yuletide holidays, fall and spring are the most popular seasons. Reservations are recommended, and be aware that parking is at a premium along the old Victorian-era carriage roads, so expect a walk, which isn't a bad thing. Consider it an opportunity to work up an appetite or walk off brunch while strolling through Tower Grove's scenic landscapes.

Tower Grove Park
4256 Magnolia Ave., St. Louis
314-575-5658
cafemadeleinestl.com

Photo credit: Café Madeline/Butler's Pantry

It's never too early to book brunch, especially during the fall and the winter holidays when the Palm House seems a little more inviting. However, if you forget to make a reservation, call and check for cancellations; a table may have opened making it your lucky day.

JOHN D. MCGURK'S

The wearing of the green is optional, since you can surround yourself with green shrubbery and plantings that decorate the fifteen-hundred-square-foot garden at John D. McGurk's Irish Pub. This urban garden includes amenities such as a multilevel deck, fountain, and waterfalls. To the delight of McGurk's patrons, tucked along the garden paths are three outdoor bars standing ready to serve garden nightlife.

The garden isn't the only place to find greens at McGurk's. Check the menu. Green salads and dishes from the Emerald Isle will make Irish eyes smile and stomachs hungry—find such specialties as bangers and mash (sausages and mashed potatoes), real Irish stew made with lamb, and the Irish-American specialty corned beef and cabbage with a side of soda bread. Other dishes, like Murphy's Irish onion gratin soup, Galway Bay crab cakes, and Irish potato chips, have a touch of Irish added to the recipe.

Ask the management what's available in the garden and they'll reply, "Anything you like." McGurk's entire menu is available in the garden, a good thing to know since inside tables get scarce when traditional Irish bands take the barroom stage. But no worries—music is piped to the garden, making hanging out and lifting a pint among the garden greenery grand.

1200 Russell Blvd., St. Louis
314-776-8309
mcgurks.com

Photo credit: John D. McGurk's

DESTINATION DINING

OVERLOOK FARM

A farm that's become an event and dining center overlooking the Mississippi River. Known for pop-up seasonal suppers, its menu depends on what's produced on the farm.

901 S Highway 79, Clarksville
573-242-3838, overlookfarmmo.com

Photo credit: Overlook Farm

DIAMOND MINERAL SPRINGS

In the 1800s, Diamond Mineral Springs was a destination spa hotel where guests came for the mineral waters, restful surroundings, and bountiful tables. It was also a time when healthy appetites were encouraged. Healthy appetites are still welcomed and are satisfied with fried chicken, chops, and fish, as the hungry gather to experience a taste of the past that the Springs has been proudly advertising as family meals since 1892.

Diamond Mineral Springs is located at a place my mother used to call a spot in the road—located about thirty minutes from the Gateway Arch near Highland, Illinois, and surrounded by farmland off Pocahontas Road in the village of Grantfork. Once there, you can decide which dining experience you want, the family-style dinner in the original hotel or fancier fare at the adjacent seasonal Back Porch. Both menus feature the Springs's famous Foot-Hi Pies.

I opt for family style and check the menu board features, usually fried or baked chicken, fish, country ham, roast pork, and dressing, and on occasion the twenty-first-century addition, flat iron steak. Soon overflowing bowls of real mashed potatoes with milk gravy, cabbage slaw, green beans, and sweet beets will arrive with your entree choice. Eat up and don't worry about the calories because you have to try the pie, especially those towering with foot-high meringue.

1 W Pocahontas Rd., Highland, IL
618-675-2655
foothipies.com

Photo credit: (top) Diamond Mineral Springs; (bottom, both) Suzanne Corbett

THE OLD BARN INN AND HEAD'S STORE AT THE INNS OF ST. ALBANS

The Old Barn Inn at The Inns of St. Albans is the heart of the European-style bed and breakfast and event center located in the historic little village of St. Albans, Missouri.

The dining outpost at the luxurious property began as a tool shed before morphing into a restaurant in an area renowned for the well-to-do.

Don't let the area's county clubs and McMansions intimidate. Stop and eat. Chances are there's room at the Old Barn's tables for its famed Sunday buffet—an affordable meal that makes a Sunday drive worthwhile. If the tables are full, take a short hop down the road to Head's Store, where breakfast, lunch, and early dinners are served Wednesday through Sunday. Head's, which opened in 1892, is listed on the National Register of Historic Places. It has served as a grocery, post office, and eatery where people can congregate for conversation and affordable burgers, sandwiches, and blue-plate-style specials. Head's can provide provisions for carryout impromptu picnics, often enjoyed lakeside across the railroad tracks from Head's patio. Others simply stop to enjoy the scenery and a dish of ice cream from Head's latest addition, the Rock Island Creamery.

Head's Store: 3516 St. Albans Rd., St. Albans
636-458-0131
innsatstalbans.com

Photo credit: The Inns at St. Albans

FAST EDDIE'S BON AIR

When Anheuser-Busch decided to open an eastside bar, they chose an Alton, Illinois, building at the crossroad triad of 4th, Pearl, and Broadway. The then-new saloon was dubbed the Bon-Air, a popular hangout from the get-go that didn't stay under brewery ownership for long. The effects of Prohibition and deregulation forced Anheuser-Busch to sell, and Sam Balaco, and later his son Lotteo, took over for the next fifty years until Eddie "Fast Eddie" Sholar acquired the taps in 1981, establishing Fast Eddie's Bon Air.

Eddie knew what people wanted—cold beer and cheap eats. Eddie delivered big time, creating a menu renowned for buck burgers and twenty-five-cents-apiece peel-and-eat boiled shrimp. Over the years prices have gone up, but hey, it's still cheap and its signature Big Elwood (steak kabobs on a stick) to date remains under four bucks.

To accommodate the ravenous and thirsty crowds, Fast Eddie's has nearly quadrupled its space, which now spills outside into a walled patio bar. If you're twenty-one or older, come on in, find a seat, and order a cold one. Don't look for any of those fancy-ass small-batch craft brews. Anheuser-Busch products still rule the taps. So grab a Bud and drink up—your food order will pop up soon.

1530 E 4th St., Alton, IL
618-462-5532
fasteddiesbonair.com

Photo credit: Fast Eddie's Bon Air

Contrary to its name, food service, especially when the place is packed, isn't fast unless you order right. To fight off hunger until that Fat Eddie Burger arrives, order the peel-and-eat shrimp. It's instant gratification, making the wait for the rest of your food order painless.

Mississippi River fishermen looking for the one that got away could possibly find that illusive catch living the good life at the Fin Inn. Built from nearby limestone and creek rocks on the Great River Road (aka Route 100) in Grafton, Illinois, the Fin Inn features fish both on and off the menu. Off-the-menu specials are the live catfish, gar, and buffalo fish swimming in the inn's eight thousand-gallon tanks. The tanks are the inn's famous attraction, and they've drawn tourists and customers since 1981, making the inn one of the favorite dinner drive destinations from St. Louis.

Take a close look. The fish on the menu are similar to those in the tanks, except that they are mostly farm raised and usually arrive tableside breaded and fried. While the fish and turtles in the tanks provide the live entertainment, it's the fish on the plate that have brought the Fin its success. On the menu are pond-raised catfish, frog legs, cod, whitefish, shrimp, clams, and buffalo fish. Buffalo fish have never been the darling of fish markets—they are usually only served at small-town fish fries and seldom make it onto a restaurant menu. Yet, buffalo fish have their fans, who claim they don't mind the bones, swearing they "melt away" during frying. Give them a try yourself at the Fin.

1500 W Main St.
Great River Road (Route 100), Grafton, IL
618-786-2030
fininn.com

Photo credit: (left) Finn Inn, (others) Visit Alton

Eat like a local. Try the fried buffalo fish sandwich or frog legs—both Mississippi River culinary classics best eaten with tartar sauce and a side of Eagles Nest Onions or a cup of Turtle Soup.

THE GRAPEVINE GRILL AT CHAUMETTE

Once upon a time, St. Louis was French and its table reflected colonial Creole flavors. After more than two hundred years, we still love our French colonial past, especially those outposts where food and wine are preserved with a Missouri French accent. Such a place is Chaumette Vineyards & Winery's Grapevine Grill, where stepping into the past begins with its location—just outside Ste. Genevieve County about forty-five minutes south on I-55.

The Grapevine Grill, housed in Chaumette's tasting room, is a room in a recreated French eighteenth-century poteaux-en-terre (vertical log) house. Owner Hank Johnson and his chef emphasize what's called a thirty-five-mile menu, sourced using ingredients produced or grown within a thirty-five-mile radius. This menu is influenced by Cajun and Creole flavors, along with other New World cuisines that are best described as New American.

When dining, seek out the cuisine du jour and the chef's specialties that incorporate wine in the recipe, such as Chaumette's bone-in Berkshire pork chop, spice-rubbed and grilled with a port wine demiglace. Whether or not your order has wine incorporated into the dish, fill your glass with one of the winery's more popular blends, such as the Huguenot Red, or a varietal like the French-oaked Chardonel, a hybrid of Chardonnay, or the Chambourcin or Vignoles—both French-American hybrids, all award winning.

24345 State Route WW, Ste. Genevieve
573-747-1000
chaumette.com

Photo credit: Chaumette Vineyards & Winery

STONE SOUP COTTAGE

Stone Soup Cottage has a secret recipe. It's a simple one: take one charming rural/farm location that's not too isolated, add a repurposed, quaint nineteenth-century cottage and barn, and combine with a James Beard-nominated chef. The result is a venue that creates upscale prix-fixe six-course dinners executed with European flare. That's been the winning recipe that chef/owner Carl McConnell and his wife, Nancy, have used to create Stone Soup Cottage. It's a formula that has made Cottleville, Missouri, a dining destination and a concept I haven't seen since the Westerfield House shuttered nearly twenty years ago in Freeburg, Illinois.

At Stone Soup Cottage, dining is enjoyed à la russe, which means that multiple courses are brought out sequentially, instead of all at once. Food is served in a charming setting where the atmosphere isn't pretentious and the dress code is relaxed. Come dressed business casual, or if you wish, dress up in a jacket and tie. Either way, you won't feel out of place.

Dinners are served Thursday through Saturday, with menus changing monthly. Book early—make that really early—because the restaurant fills up a month in advance. If there isn't a place at the table, consider booking space at one of Stone Soup Cottage's cooking classes. Classes feature three recipes from the current month's menu. It's the win-win experience for me. Learn a few great recipes while sampling the cuisine without the dinner reservation.

5809 Highway N, Cottleville
636-244-2233
stonesoupcottage.com

Photo credit: Stone Soup Cottage

TIENDA EL RANCHITO MEXICAN RESTAURANT & GROCERY STORE

The search for authentic Mexican food and groceries doesn't have to involve crossing the southern border. Instead, cross over the Mississippi to Fairview Heights, Illinois, where El Ranchito offers a one-stop shop—a grocery/meat market, restaurant, and bar.

Don't let Tienda El Ranchito's location and unassuming building fool you; it's a larger operation than it appears. Once inside you'll encounter the grocery section, where customers shop for staples, and the fresh meat counter, where specialty cuts such as spiced fajita meat and homemade chorizo are made fresh daily. Follow the grocery aisles accented with hanging piñatas and shop the assortment that ranges from imported canned goods and candies to breads and cornhusks. Brush up on your high school Spanish or ask for help translating, since the lables of many items are printed in Spanish.

To find the restaurant, follow the grocery aisles to the back of the store to a small hallway, which opens into the restaurant, where the camp Mexican décor is as inviting as the smells from the kitchen. Customers can eat early, beginning with breakfast and a plateful of *huevos* con chorizo or *chilaquiles*, dishes available throughout the day. For a heartier lunch or dinner, survey the menu and pick from Tex-Mex to house *especiales* created from family recipes, homemade sauces, and meats taken from the grocery's counters.

2565 N 32nd St., Fairmont City, IL
618-875-1521
tiendaelranchito.com

Photo credit: Tienda El Ranchito

After indulging in plates made with Tienda El Ranchito
own custom cut meats and sausages you may be inspired
to visit the meat counter on the way out. So bring a cooler
and stock it for the ride home. Just top those meats with
ice, which can also be bought on site.

CEDAR LAKE CELLARS

If a Napa Valley wine experience isn't in the budget, I suggest taking a short drive down I-70 to Wright City (about forty minutes from St. Louis) and following the back roads to Cedar Lake Cellars. The winery and event center with a twentieth-century farm theme is the brainchild of owner Carl Bolm. The complex occupies 170-plus acres, including its namesake, a three-acre lake where guests are welcome to sip and savor the surroundings.

Cedar Lake Cellars is unlike any Missouri winery—it's not a traditional winery where wine is made and cellared. It offers more than just Missouri wines. Check the shelves and you'll find that Cedar Lake's wine stock includes domestic and international bottles from twenty-five different wine regions. It also features 3 Swans, its own elite label and collection that could impress a sommelier.

Where there's wine, there's food, and Cedar Lake's food venues are as impressive as their wine selections. Lakeside Grill's smoked meat sandwiches create grab-and-go platters perfect for lounging the day away around the lake. The winery's tasting bar and dining room provide casual upscale cuisine that's locally sourced, featuring seafood, steaks, and handmade pastas. Cedar Lake's best bet? Their themed events, which include wine dinners and seasonal flings with the occasional hog roast throw-downs paired with evening fireworks.

11008 Schreckengast Rd., Wright City
636-745-9500
cedarlakecellars.com

Photo credit: Cedar Lake Cellars

GLASSES AND MUGS

ANHEUSER-BUSCH

Anheuser-Busch Beermaster Tour. The tour that goes beyond the complimentary tour and hospitality suite's free beer. Guests get to trek through the historic Brew House, Lager Cellar, and Finishing Cellar for samples directly from the tank, along with a beer-making crash course.

1200 Lynch St., St. Louis, 314-577-2626

Photo credit: Suzanne Corbett

ROBUST

S ip, sample, and shop. That's the mantra of Robust, the quaint little
wine bar, eatery, and gift shop that first opened its doors in the
St. Louis County suburb of Webster Groves. At the time, this was
a unique concept, one that has since been copied many times over,
proving the old adage, "Imitation is the sincerest form of flattery."
Robust's popularity also fueled its own expansion downtown next
to the America's Center Convention Complex. This location, which
offers most of the wine selections found in Webster Groves, is great
for downtowners and tourists. Nonetheless, I prefer the original
location, a bistro-like setting tucked in a strip center along the west
edge of Lockwood Avenue near Straub's.

As with any good bistro, there are sidewalk tables, the choice place
to sip and indulge in conversation. If the weather's uncooperative
for the sidewalk, step inside and step up to the oversized wine bar,
or snag a table, where you'll be exposed to the Robust Factor—aka
the wine selection guide. It's the best, most customer-friendly menu
guide I've ever seen, dividing wines into non-intimidating categories:
Bubbles, Mellow, Luscious, Generous, Soft-Hearted, Sweet &
Stickies, and of course, Robust. It's an approach novices can embrace,
while it produces chuckles from the wine savvy. Look for the wine
flights, a grouping of several wine pours that are presented with the
same fun flair. My favorite is Robust's red wine flight entitled "In
Bed with Red."

227 W Lockwood Ave., Webster Groves
314-963-0033
robustwinebar.com

Photo credit: (left) Suzanne Corbett; (right, both) Robust

Every Wednesday is Flight Night. It's a great way to save some cash while sipping your way through wines that normally wouldn't be on your radar. If you discover a wine you can't live without, go shop the back of the house where wine flight wines are available by the bottle.

URBAN CHESTNUT BREWING COMPANY

Beer and St. Louis. It's the ultimate matchup, and it hasn't changed since the 19th century, when neighborhood breweries dotted the urban landscape and before Prohibition drained the taps. That tradition has been rekindled thanks to brewmasters like Florian Kuplent, co-owner of Urban Chestnut Brewing Company, a St. Louis craft brewery that now numbers three locations. Brewing 25 different varieties, Urban Chestnut describes its beer styles as New World meets Old World, a concept that Urban Chestnut calls Beer Divergency—a mission to create modern American beers while embracing brewing heritage.

Beer Divergency is what has driven the constant development and testing of new brews at Urban Chestnut's URB (Urban Research Brewery), where casual beer drinkers and self-proclaimed beer connoisseurs can show up Wednesdays through Sundays for the opportunity to sample three two-ounce pours of its latest beers for a buck. The catch? Drink up and fill out a feedback survey.

Looking for more than an experimental two-ounce sample? To imbibe in full glasses and steins, just cross the street to Urban Chestnut's spacious bierhall, the closest thing to a Munich-style bierhall you'll find this side of the Mississippi. Find a seat at one of the communal tables and order up. Choose from the Revolution series (craft artisanal modern American beers) or the Reverence series (European-styled heritage brews)—all of which pair nicely with schnitzel, wurst, or pretzels.

Photo credit: Urban Chestnut Brewing Company

Party like a German in Urban Chestnut's Midtown Brewery Biergarten during the outdoor season. Look for events such as its Blues and BBQ summer series. Otherwise take a tour, self-guided or guided. Opt for the guided Saturday tour, which includes a generous sample and requires as reservation.

URB (Urban Research Brewery)
4501 Manchester Ave., St. Louis

UC Grove Brewery & Bierhall
4465 Manchester Ave., St. Louis

314-222-0143
urbanchestnut.com

SQUARE ONE BREWERY AND DISTILLERY

Square One took the term "housemade" to a higher level when it opened as a microbrewery restaurant in 2006. Beyond the normal menu and beers of an upscale gastropub, Square One stocks its back bar with its own spirits created by its own stillhouse, branded under Spirits of St. Louis. Considering that Square One was one of St. Louis's earliest craft brewers, it was no surprise that its owners took the leap to become Missouri's first microdistillery since Prohibition. So belly up to the bar and take a look.

To date there are twenty-one different spirits along with a dozen brews on tap to wet one's whistle. One of those spirited concoctions is Scandinavia-inspired aquavit. It is a rare libation whose dominant flavor is caraway, with notes of fennel, dill, cumin, and cardamom—a versatile liquor that is well served neat, on the rocks, or as a mixer.

I'm a whiskey girl, so I was attracted to Square One's single malt whiskey, J. J. Neukomm. It's a smooth drink with a faint taste of smoke achieved from its cherrywood-smoked malt, making it a good chaser to almost any of Square One's ever-growing catalog of beers. To optimize your tasting experience, pick a dish from the menu that uses beer or spirits in the recipe, then pair it with what's filling your glass.

1727 Park Ave., St. Louis
314-231-2537
squareonebrewery.com

Photo credit: Square One Brewery and Distillery

PLANTER'S HOUSE

The success of Planter's House is distilled from the past, one that celebrates St. Louis's cocktail tradition established at the old Planter's Hotel (1817–1922), home of the famous Planter's Punch and where Jerry Thomas, considered the grandfather of American mixology, tended bar. In homage to this history and driven by renewed appreciation of craft cocktails, the new Planter's House has become a destination for hipsters and bons vivants seeking edgier new libations and retro classics.

Housed in vintage rehabbed digs in Lafayette Square, the exposed brick and rich woodwork at Planter's House contribute to its cozy classic atmosphere—enhancing the experience as a maraschino cherry does a manhattan. Once inside, the challenge begins. The happy customer must choose from nearly seventy handcrafted cocktails, which are divided into four categories: Planter's House Cocktails, New Classics, House Classics such as Planter's Punch, and House Favorites featuring such retro drinks as mint juleps. The adventurous will want to try the mixologist's current darling, amaro cocktails, which are kissed with a variety of bitters.

Non-spirit drinkers can opt to fill a glass with wine or bubbles from a limited yet substantive wine list. Of course, there is always beer. A dozen local craft beers are served alone or as the foil for what Planter's calls "Beer and Bond"—a beer with a shot, or what old-timers called boilermakers.

1000 Mississippi Ave., St. Louis
314-696-2603
plantershousestl.com

Photo credit: Planter's House

If you come for cocktails, stay for the food. While it's easy to focus on how Planter's House will fill your glass, consider what the chefs can do to fill your plate. Even if your appetite is light, make room for the chef's snacks and appetizers.

Size matters. And that doesn't necessarily translate to bigger is better. Depending on where you are, a small place can be a big deal. That's the case at Tiny Bar, a must-stop for Cardinals fans before home games. Granted, the Tiny Bar's gimmick is its diminutive size—just 250 square feet including a closet and lobby. Tiny Bar was created in honor of Eddie Gaedel, the three-foot-seven-inch tall St. Louis Browns baseball player whose jersey number was 1/8. Eddie made only one appearance at the plate, where he drew a walk. That appearance is memorialized on Tiny Bar's limited wall space.

While Tiny Bar and Gaedel are small, the bar's drinks are regular sized. Many of its crafty libations carry through the tiny theme with drinks named the Villechaize, the Yellow Brick Road, and the Marteenee. Patrons under five feet tall and of legal drinking age are eligible for the five-foot special—twenty-five percent off their tab.

If you ever want to eat at Tiny Bar, forget it. Plan on ballpark concessions because there's little room for a chip rack, let alone a kitchen. But that's not what makes Tiny Bar unique. It's all about the lack of space and the crush of the crowd, which according to the fire marshal, can't exceed twenty. Tiny Bar, a hangout for Cards fans, is simply a place to grab a cool one and sit and relax, provided there's a place to sit.

1008 Locust Ave., St. Louis
314-478-9833
tinybarstl.com

Photo credit: Tiny Bar

SUMP COFFEE

Coffee seasonality isn't something the majority of coffee drinkers consider. Freshness has been defined by roast, brewing method, and how long it has been sitting in the pot. That's changing, thanks to Sump Coffee, which only deals in seasonal, single-sourced coffees. For example, Central American and Colombian coffees are available in spring, while African coffees such as Ethiopian and Kenyan and those from the Indonesian island chain are winter brews.

Care is taken not to spill these beans—meaning single origins aren't blended together. Beans are separately handled and generally given a light roast to maintain the integrity of origin and their original natural flavor profiles. Flavor profiles described as floral, spice, dark fruit, light body, and soft sound like wine descriptors but are an apt fit for Sump's coffee.

Cups are filled with traditionally brewed coffee served black. If you need sugar (not artificial sweeteners) or milk (not cream), you'll have to ask for them. They're kept behind the counter. Just like chefs who keep salt and pepper shakers off the table, Sump wants customers to taste the coffee first before reaching for add-ins. As an FYI, while you'll find milk in the espresso drinks like cortado, cappuccino, latte, and dirty chai, don't look for syrups, caramel, or pumpkin spice. Remember Sump's motto: It's just coffee—no frills.

3700 S Jefferson Ave., St. Louis
917-412-5670
sumpcoffee.com

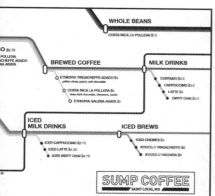

Photo credit: (top) Jim Corbett III (left) Suzanne Corbett; (right) Sump Coffee

SKI SODA & EXCEL BOTTLING

Throwback sodas made with real cane sugar are a blast from the past that Excel Bottling has excelled in making for more than eighty years. Actually, you can't really call Excel's sodas throwbacks, since they have never stopped making their sodas the way they always have, following original recipes from the 1930s. Back then, the most popular soda pop flavors from regional bottlers were root beer, black cherry, orange, and Ski, the citrus-flavored soda whose recipe hails from Tennessee and is often compared to Mountain Dew.

Excel has had the franchise to produce Ski at its Breese, Illinois, bottling plant since 1961, and the lemony-orangey drink remains a star among Excel's stable of sodas. Its varieties now number eighteen and include Lucky Cola and retro classics such as Frostie Root Beer, Million Dollar Grape, and Red Cream. All sodas are sweetened the old-school way with real cane sugar, never high-fructose corn syrup, and bottled in glass like the ones we rinsed out and returned for a two-cent deposit.

Ski and its sister sodas are available throughout St. Louis at area groceries and liquor stores. If you're lucky, you can get one of Excel's sodas on draft. As any true-blue soda jerk would attest, draft soda tastes best, so look around, especially at eateries sourcing local products, and chances are you'll find Ski, Lucky, and Frostie on draft.

488 S Broadway, Breese, IL
618-526-7159
excelbottling.com

Photo credit: Excel Bottling Company

BALABAN'S

Winning five Wine Spectator Awards of Excellence and five more Best of Awards of Excellence is no easy task. It takes expertise to create a wine program that is both satisfying and diverse for the consumer. That's exactly what Balaban's has achieved. In fact, wine and wine pairings have been its focus from the get-go, dating back to 1972 at its Central West End location. After thirty-seven years in the CWE, Balaban's made the decision to move to Chesterfield Valley, where it continues to build on its reputation, redefining itself as a wine shop and bistro. Look around. There's an impressive inventory that numbers more than six hundred domestic and international bottles, including rare library finds. Balaban's wines complement the bistro menu and the wine dinner series, which is designed for the enjoyment of both wine novices and serious foodies.

Sharing shelf space on the back bar are craft beers and boutique/small-batch spirits such as Angel's Envy port barrel finished bourbon that's been finished in French oak port barrels. Spirits and brews aside, wine rules Balaban's, where wine suggestions are included on the menu along with the wine bar's affordable by-the-glass wine program. It's the best way to discover and sample without having to buy a bottle.

1772 Clarkson Rd., Chesterfield
636-449-6700
balabanswine.com

Photo credit: Balaban's

GLOBAL GRUB

LONA'S LIL EATS

Chinese with a touch of soul is its culinary mantra. A small place with big flavors and home of the Giant Rice Paper Wrap.

2199 California Ave., St. Louis
314-925-8938, lonaslileats.com

Photo credit: Lona's Lil Eats

PHO GRAND

Over the years, I've found that a restaurant's entrance often foreshadows the dining experience. Pho Grand is such a place— its elevated portico sets it apart from its South Grand neighbors. Climb the front steps, step into the small dining room, and take a quick look at the menu. You'll soon expect big things from the kitchen: authentic Vietnamese dishes, many of which were first introduced to the city by Pho Grand. As the first Vietnamese restaurant to open in St. Louis, the restaurant contributed to the transformation of South Grand as a dining destination for international flavors. Until Pho Grand, St. Louis's exposure to Asian cuisines was mainly limited to Chinese buffets and the occasional sushi bar.

First-timers to the cuisine often begin their exploration with pho, the restaurant's namesake. Pho is a hearty beef broth and noodle soup flavored with aromatics such as lemongrass and cilantro and served in oversized bowls. Partner those pho bowls with one or more of the country's more interesting first courses, including steamed rice paper spring rolls, called goi cuon, or an exotic lotus root salad. Curious diners and those in the know order banh cuon, or rice flour crepes. Banh cuon is an excellent example of the culinary cultural collision between the Vietnamese and the French, who occupied the southeast Asian nation for decades. These dishes, now considered authentic Vietnamese cuisine, make Pho Grand unique.

3195 South Grand Blvd., St. Louis
314-664-7435
phogrand.com

Photo credit: Pho Grand

MILAGRO MODERN MEXICAN

Finding a modern take on Mexican food isn't easy when the culinary landscape is awash with generic Tex-Mex menus that push oversized margaritas and combo plates with refried beans and rice. Within the last few years, alternatives have surfaced—a standout among the more inspired cantinas is Milagro Modern Mexican. It's not an easy place to find, tucked near the back side of the Shoppes in Old Webster off West Lockwood down a side parking lot. Just don't give up if your GPS can't find it, because you'll be rewarded with Milagro's creative, updated take on traditional regional Mexican dishes.

Milagro's menu and dining concept are the brainchild of two siblings, Jason and Adam Tilford, who know a thing or two about taking Mexican food to the next level. These guys helped redefine Mexican food in The Lou with Mission Taco Joints and Mission Food Truck, proving once and for all that there are countless ways to tastefully stuff a taco.

Milagro's menu and atmosphere design aim to create an experience similar to what you might have in an upscale restaurant in Mexico instead of a "Mexican" restaurant. Considering Milagro's off-the-beaten-path location, edgy dishes like cochinita pibil (achiote-rubbed pork braised in banana leaves) and agave tequila cocktails, that mission is accomplished.

20 Allen Ave. #130, St. Louis
314-962-4300
milagromodernmexican.com

Photo credit: (top left) Suzanne Corbett; (top right, bottom) Milagro Modern Mexican

Sure bets aren't usually found on a casino floor— unless you're at the Ameristar St. Charles Casino trolling for your next meal. One such bet is Asia, tucked along the casino floor's back side beyond the slots and gaming tables. Asia, an affordable upscale eatery, features traditional and contemporary Chinese and Vietnamese dishes. Forget the buffet line—everything at Asia is cooked to order, fresh from the wok, and served in Asia's sleek dining room designed to make both high rollers and nickel slots patrons happy.

Menu choices are a combination of American-Chinese favorites (think General Tso's chicken and crab Rangoon) and traditional regional specialties such as salt and pepper shrimp and Vietnamese pho bowls. Counted among Asia's contemporary plates are the Szechuan pepper-laced hot chili catfish and the lemongrass wings, fried wings enrobed with a sweet lemongrass glaze and garnished with crisp shallots and Thai basil.

Asia's chefs have extensively researched the recipes to ensure genuine flavor. To further stack the odds in the kitchen's favor, Ameristar's top chef, Don Yamauchi, brought chef de cuisine Hai-Ying Bushey, a native of Guangzhou, China, to oversee the menu, resulting in a big win, but not for everyone. There is a catch. To indulge yourself at Asia, you must be twenty-one or older—no one under twenty-one is allowed on the casino floor.

Ameristar Casino Resort Spa St. Charles
1 Ameristar Blvd.
636-949-7777
ameristar.com/st-charles/asia

Photo credit: Ameristar Casino Resort Spa St. Charles

ASSUMPTION GREEK ORTHODOX CHURCH'S FRIDAY GREEK LUNCH

Greek mythology calls ambrosia the food of the gods. At Assumption Greek Orthodox Church in West St. Louis County, heavenly food fit for the gods is served each Friday.

Assumption's cooks have a mantra—if you cook they will come and eat. And they have. Assumption's Friday feast, considered West County's ultimate pop-up lunch, is a fundraiser that began twenty years ago when the church's ladies started cooking. That led to a sign posted on Assumption's front lawn stating "Greek Lunch Today."

Greek lunches feature homemade traditional Greek dishes such as moussaka, gyros, spanakopita, and baklava. All are made fresh and with all the TLC any yia-yia (Greek for "grandmother") would provide. Fact is, I can easily count several grandmothers among Assumption's lunch volunteers who have cooked and worked the lunch for years. They offer guests a tip—check the menu before you come. It does have minor week-to-week change-ups and can include special entrees such as lamb shanks now and then. You can always tell when lamb shanks hit the menu because the lunch line gets long fast, and they sell out within the first hour. That's no surprise, considering Assumption serves 800 to 1,500 lunches each Friday. Of course, grabbing a carryout is faster, but stick around and dine in if you can. The atmosphere is as savory as the food.

1755 Des Peres Rd., St. Louis
314-966-6720
assumptiongoc.org/friday-lunch

Photo credit: Assumption Greek Orthodox Church

Plan to arrive early for lamb shanks or other popular lunch specials. These items sell out fast. And if lines are long consider the carryout option. Dining al fresco via an impromptu lunch on the lawn can be delightful.

ST. RAYMOND'S MARONITE CATHEDRAL'S CEDARS BANQUET HALL WEDNESDAY LEBANESE LUNCH

Walk past St. Raymond's on Mondays and Tuesdays and you'll smell—and maybe catch a glimpse of—what its legions of volunteers are cooking.

Meat pies are getting folded, grape leaves are being stuffed and rolled, and pastries are baking in preparation for St. Raymond's legendary Wednesday lunch. It's been the ultimate place to power-lunch for decades for politicians, cops, and the business elite, who gather to strategize countless deals and discuss public policy over plates of fried football-shaped kibbi, tabouli, and cups of Lebanese coffee. Politics aside, those who come each Wednesday usually don't come to power-lunch. They're here for the food and a menu that hasn't changed much over decades.

Beyond the savory, the menu sports traditional homemade Lebanese and Middle Eastern-style pastries cooked and baked using time-honored family recipes. In consideration of the non-adventurous or picky eaters, there are a few American menu options, such as chicken and dumplings, a regular that's always on St. Ray's cafeteria line.

Photo credit: St. Raymond's Maronite Cathedral

Arrive early to get the best choices and to avoid the noontime rush. While the lunch line can be long, it moves fast, and communal round tables are plentiful. So take a seat, eat up, and look around. Your table may be next to the mayor.

931 Lebanon Drive, St. Louis
314-621-0056
straymond-mc.org

AL-TARBOUSH DELI

$\mathcal{S}$troll along the Loop's Walk of Fame and take a detour at Westgate. Just a few yards away is Al-Tarboush Deli, a favorite of students, foodies, and the Loop savvy. When it opened twenty years ago as a Mediterranean deli, few understood the concept—most thought its specialty was Italian—forgetting that the Mediterranean is the crossroads to three continents and more than a dozen cuisines. Al-Tarboush helped enlighten and change St. Louis's culinary landscape with its deli quick-mart Middle Eastern and Greek specialties that weren't only unique but affordably priced.

The charm of Al-Tarboush is the building's layout. It's far from fancy. I'd even call it barebones, with only a few tables inside and along the sidewalk. Grocery racks and a cooler line the walls along with the deli cold case that morphs into the order counter. Step up and survey the case. Look for the day's selection of savory pies and pastries, then check out the hummus, baba ghanoush, and tabbouleh—great as lunch add-ons or as take-home sides to indulge with or without an order of falafel.

The menu isn't large, but it's diverse, offering appetizers, salads, sandwiches, hand pies, and desserts. Shish taouk is my top pick, with marinated chicken breast, garlic paste, and a dill pickle, wrapped in flatbread and toasted crisp. Shawarma fans won't be disappointed, nor will those craving gyros, which are available with beef, lamb, or chicken, an option I haven't seen outside Greece.

602 Westgate Ave., St. Louis
314-725-1944
altarboushdeliuniversitycity.com

Photo credit: (left) Jim Corbett III, (right, both) Al-Tarboush Deli

Seating is limited but table turnover fast. While waiting for a table to clear shop the cold cases. They're filled with plenty of savory items, including an assortment of pastries perfect to add to your dinner menu.

THE SCOTTISH ARMS

Scottish pubs may appear to resemble Irish or British public (pub) houses—delightfully dark and cozy and staffed with friendly bartenders who man the taps. Places where friends gather and the pints flow freely. However, the Scottish difference can be summed up in two words, food and Scotch. Food beyond the haggis and a collection of nearly two hundred Scotch whiskys are what define Ally Nisbet's Scottish Arms, St. Louis's only Scottish-themed pub.

Survey the single malt and blended Scotch whiskys displayed before just bellying up to the ornate vintage wooden bar. Each will have its own distinct character, and you may have to do a little sampling to discover what you like. Perhaps you're not a Scotch drinker—then take stock of the beer taps for Scottish beers along with a grand assortment of international ales, porters, and ciders, along with domestic craft brews.

Once your glass is full, fill your plate. Haddock, cold smoked salmon, and haggis fritters balance the menu with such eclectic choices as venison, mussels, and shaved duck burnt ends. As for pub grub, consider the Scotch eggs, Celtic crisps (potato chips) with curry dip, and bangers and mash, or my favorite to down with a pint, Forfar bridies—the lighter Scottish take on meat pies—a rare find on any menu.

8 S Sarah St.., St. Louis
314-535-0551
thescottisharms.com

Photo credit: Suzanne Corbett

Years ago, when Bailey Farms Dairy shuttered its south St. Louis City operation, I mourned the loss. Little did I know that I would later rejoice when the building, found within the Bevo Mill area that's affectionately been called Little Sarajevo, was repurposed for Grbic, one of St. Louis's most celebrated Bosnian restaurants.

Grbic is a mom-and-pop operation established by Ermina and Sulejman Grbic, who together brought a wealth of culinary expertise and family recipes from their native Yugoslavia. Ermina serves as executive chef, while Sulejman personally oversees all the meat selection and cutting. Daughter Senada, a graduate of Le Cordon Bleu culinary school, worked side by side with her mother to recreate dishes reflecting the Bosnian region. Some are surprisingly familiar, such as the German-influenced Wiener Schnitzel, and Jäger Schnitzel, topped with mushroom sauce, a Bosnian favorite, and served with housemade spaetzles.

Balkan menu standouts include ćevapi, or beef sausages; sarma, or paprika-sauced stuffed cabbage rolls; and baked Valdostana—layers of spaetzles, sliced beef, mushroom sauce, and cheese. Many discover that Bosnian food is an amalgam of culinary cultures including Greek, Italian, and Middle Eastern, so order up and explore the menu. Just save room for a slice of tiramisu, strudel, or the Balkan chocolate cream crêpe, palačinke, with a Bosnian coffee.

4071 Keokuk St., St. Louis
314-772-3100
grbicrestaurant.com

Grbić
Restaurant &
Banquet Hall

PLATES
WITH
A PAST

BEVO MILL

Das Bevo: Bevo Mill, another culinary landmark born from Anheuser-Busch, lives again as Das Bevo, open and embracing its German heritage and its extraordinary biergarten.

4749 Gravois Ave., St. Louis
314-224-5521, dasbevo.com

Photo credit: Suzanne Corbett

TONY'S

Classy never goes out of style. I still adore tabletops draped with white starched linens, set with real silver flatware and fresh flowers. Back in the day, white tablecloths were the norm, and elegant tables, beautiful décor, and stellar service defined fine dining. Those elements still define fine dining for me, as they do at Tony's, where silver place settings and tableside service rules. Tony's has a style that matches its contemporary Continental menu and the eatery continues to maintain its legendary dining experience with only one change—the suspension of its coat and tie requirement. The transition to casual business attire that I'll call "relaxed chic" is an unavoidable sign of the times.

Transitioning is nothing new for Tony's. After all, food service, dining styles, and culinary trends always change, and Tony's has mastered its evolution since it first opened as a humble spaghetti house decades ago. Vince Bommarito Sr. was a teenager when he stepped up to the plate to run the restaurant after his father's death, transforming the spaghetti house into a steakhouse and then into a classic five-star restaurant with an international reputation.

Today, the third generation of Bommaritos have taken Tony's helm. Vince Jr. continues Tony's classic elegance through its menu and core commitments to quality and style. Expect to be indulged and tempted with its menu, renowned for chops, shellfish, Dover sole, prime steaks, and of course, homemade pasta.

410 Market St., St. Louis
314-231-7007
tonysstlouis.com

Photo credit: Tony's

Prepare to be pampered and to dine leisurely; don't rush through dinner. Tony's is a place where classic table service seasons the experience. While the dress code has relaxed, dress up anyway and arrive in style.

AL'S RESTAURANT

Roll along the riverfront north of the Gateway Arch and you'll discover—or perhaps rediscover—Al's, St. Louis's oldest single-family-run restaurant, which has been at the same location since 1925. To find it, look for its neon sign, which serves as a beacon at First Street and Biddle. The sign has been attached to the remains of a nineteenth-century sugar warehouse and early-twentieth-century saloon since Al and Louise Barroni bought the premises in 1925. Back then, the menu focused on cold beer, Louise's egg sandwiches, and hot lunches dished from steam tables cafeteria-style.

Soon after Al Jr. took over, the building next door caught fire. That's when the menu and dining room got a makeover, becoming a steakhouse and a famed riverboat bar made from steamboat deck planks and painted with a riverfront mural by a set designer from The Muny. It was also about this time that Al's lost the menu—so listen up. They don't have printed menus. Servers recite the menu with a show-and-tell cart filled with steaks, chops, and seafood, explaining the various preparations of each minus the price tags. Don't be shy; ask the prices, otherwise you could be surprised. Al's is pricey. But what the heck . . . you're dining where Frank Sinatra dined with his dog. No joke. And for the record, two steaks were ordered.

1200 N First St., St. Louis
314-421-6399
alsrestaurant.net

Photo credit: Al's Restaurant

History rules at Al's so take the time to experience the vintage atmosphere. Have a drink in the Riverboat lounge and call ahead and request the Sinatra table.

DRESSEL'S PUBLIC HOUSE

Dressel's past could be best described as cultural "terroir," a term, often used when discussing wine, that translates to a sense of place, community, and environment. Such is Dressel's, a blast from the past reminiscent of St. Louis circa 1960, when the CWE was a bohemian haven and nearby Gaslight Square rocked. Dressel's was inspired by the owners' time living in Wales, but they don't consider it a Welsh "themed" pub. Rather, the website states that it is "an organic expression of a relationship with two places—1960s St. Louis and Gaslight Square."

OK, I still call it themed. It still has classic pub design with décor featuring dead poets, writers, and composers cluttering its walls, inviting surroundings appealing to a clientele ranging from millennials to aging hippies to surviving beatniks. Dressel's menu also attracts the culinarily curious.

The menu has evolved over the decades to combine old pub fare with a farm-to-table concept. It's a pleasing culinary collision, and the chefs have upped the ante with creations of their own like lamb burgers dressed with apricot chutney and chèvre. Not quite the pub grub you're looking for? Relax, there are old-school burgers, fish and chips, and truffled grilled cheese and tomato bisque, recognized as a menu standout by the Food Network.

419 N Euclid Ave., St. Louis
314-361-1060
dresselspublichouse.com

Photo credit: Dressel's Public House

THE FEASTING FOX

Germans have a name for it—*gemütlichkeit*. Loosely translated, that's a combination of friendliness and good times. *Gemütlichkeit*, as defined in south St. Louis by the Feasting Fox, is good times served with German food and beer. It's a tradition that began in 1914 when beer baron August Busch Sr. opened the half-timbered Bavarian-styled Gretchen's Inn as a respectable family restaurant where beer could be enjoyed.

Antitrust laws forced Busch to divest himself from the operation, so he leased it to a buddy, Al Smith, who operated it as Al Smith's Bavarian Inn, a name that stuck through its closure in 1986. Old-timers continue to call it simply Al Smith's, which is OK since the Feasting Fox still flourishes and continues the *gemütlichkeit* tradition. A testament to the restaurant's tenacity, surviving Prohibition, a fire, management changes, and the near-destruction of the historic building. It still provides south St. Louis with German culinary specialties such as sauerbraten and schnitzel, which has become a signature item. Make that "items," because there are four different schnitzels, ranging from the egg-crowned Holsteiner to the earthy, mushroom-sauced Jäger style plated with spaetzle, sauerkraut, or potato pancakes. These traditional sides can give the menu's ausländer (non-German) entrees such as steaks, chops, and burgers a subtle German accent.

4200 S Grand Blvd., St. Louis
314-352-3500
feastingfox.com

Photo credit: The Feasting Fox

THE TENDERLOIN ROOM

Clubby, snappy, and stylish—that's how I define this mid-century modern American steakhouse, renowned for charcoal broilers and carnivorous clientele. At The Tenderloin Room, diners can find dark wood paneling, comfy chairs, and tuxedo-clad waiters serving succulent, stylish meals. It's at The Tenderloin Room at the Chase Park Plaza that the likes of the Rat Pack dined, the steaks sizzled, and Hack's Hellenic salads (named for the restaurant's famed maître d') were tossed. In its heyday, The Tenderloin was considered the place to be seen and catch a glimpse of Hollywood celebrities, often registered guests at the Chase.

Stars still appear on occasion, just not as often as they once did. And over the years, The Tenderloin Room has had its ups and downs—a devastating fire in 1968 and a rebuild and relaunch in 1970, before finally closing in 1991. However, the grand old dame wasn't shuttered long, thanks to the Karagiannis family—of Spiro's fame—who refurbished and reopened the landmark in 1993.

Once again Greek (Hellenic) salads and its fabled signature Pepperloin à la Tenderloin are back on the menu to satisfy the cravings of sophisticated carnivores. To enjoy dining as it used to be in the 1960s, order a shrimp cocktail and finish dinner with cherries jubilee. It will be a taste of the past and a nod to The Tenderloin Room's tradition.

232 N Kingshighway Blvd., St. Louis
314-361-0900
tenderloinroom.com

Photo credit: The Tenderloin Room

CROWN CANDY KITCHEN

Candy, ice cream, and BLT sandwiches keep the petite dining room at Crown Candy packed, as lines for tables spill out the door and down the sidewalk. Customers don't seem to mind. They've been lining up for Crown Candy's confections and lunches since 1913, when Greek confectioners Harry Karandzieff and Peter Jugaloff set up shop on the city's north side.

Over the years, nothing much has changed. Crown still has its wooden and glass display cases and small booths, which were the original store fixtures. Coca-Cola memorabilia, assorted photographs, and knickknacks line the walls along with an oversized menu board, which reflects the only real changes in the restaurant's hundred-year history—the prices.

Stuff yourself into one of those vintage booths and plan on stuffing yourself. Start with one or more of Crown's customer favorites, like chili and tamales or the killer BLT on Wonder Bread spread with Miracle Whip, the very BLT proclaimed as one of the Food Network's best sandwiches in America. As for me, I scream for Crown's ice cream, perhaps a Johnny Rabbitt Special (fresh banana malt with pecans and nutmeg) or a World's Fair sundae. Wait, I'll take a Newport. That's a sundae with a ton of whipped cream and chopped pecans, and then I'll get a pound of chocolate-covered peanut clusters to take home.

1401 St. Louis Ave., St. Louis
314-621-9650
crowncandykitchen.net

Photo credit: Crown Candy Kitchen

CHARCOAL HOUSE

Driving west along Manchester Road, I feel like I'm traveling through time, so to speak. The time warp hits around the 10-mile mark from the Mississippi, where, starting in 1906, stood the Ten Mile House. The place is still there, surviving today as the Charcoal House. The changeover occurred in 1957, when Manchester was a less-traveled road. To get customers to travel a little further down the road, it was thought that charcoal-grilled steaks would bring the hungry to its door. The plan worked.

Charcoal-grilled steaks still get customers to stop in to eat in a dining room that's changed little, from the décor to the menu, since the 1970s. This is a good thing for foodies who delight in classic American steakhouse food served in an atmosphere some might call kitschy, while others, including myself, would simply call nostalgic. Either way, it doesn't matter because what has made the Charcoal House a destination over time remains its original charbroiled steaks—Black Angus twenty-eight-day wet-aged filets and sirloins, hand cut and custom grilled, and garnished with a french-fried onion ring, the high-end garnish of its day. To get the onion ring topper, order your Filet à la George, named for George Angelos, who, with his brother Steve, owns the place and keeps the charbroiler flames burning.

9855 Manchester Rd., Rock Hill
314-968-4842
charcoalhousestl.com

Photo credit: Charcoal House

Take note of the olive oil. Charcoal House produces
their own Kalamata olive oil from family olive groves in
Kalamata, Greece, from trees over five hundred years old.

BIG CHIEF

Anyone who traveled through St. Louis on Route 66 since 1929 knew the Big Chief was the place to eat and sleep. The Big Chief's motel has vanished along with the traffic from the old route, but the hacienda-style restaurant building, now listed on the National Register of Historic Places, has been restored and reinvented, and the staff is still cooking meals to feed hungry travelers.

The Big Chief, while revamped, still takes pride in its past. Just like the old roadhouse, the food is affordable, with a full-service menu combining old and new roadside favorites, including a selection of house-smoked meats. You can often catch a sweet smell of the smoke from the parking lot.

Big Chief's kitchen favorites are as diverse as the travelers who drove the route. An eclectic menu features road-food classics such as southwestern country fried steak done right—flattened, hand-breaded, and sized to nearly cover the plate. Something else that catches the eye is a chef's creation you won't find anywhere else, the toasted lasagna, which is rolled, breaded, and deep-fried. It's plated upright in a pool of roasted garlic cream and pomodoro sauces. Sauces are made from tomatoes and basil grown in a 9,000-square-foot garden—the ultimate repurposing of the space that once occupied the old Big Chief's motel cabins.

17352 Manchester Rd., Wildwood
636-458-3200
bigchiefstl.com

Photo credit: (left) Big Chief; (center) Suzanne Corbett; (right) Big Chief

MARKETS AND FARM STANDS

VIVIANO'S

Viviano's Festa Italiano is a place for Italian food fans who seek authentic ingredients and a good lunch along with Italian products. It's a little piece of The Hill in southwest and west St. Louis County where Italian cravings can be satisfied.

62 Fenton Plaza, Fenton, 636-305-1474
150 Four Seasons Plaza, Chesterfield, 314-878-1474
vivianosmarket.com

Photo credit: Suzanne Corbett

THE SMOKEHOUSE MARKET

Surviving country stores and butcher shops have charm, especially those that sell produce, fresh meats, and staples. Such is the old Chesterfield Mercantile Company, now The Smokehouse Market, whose evolution has taken it from a downhome country meat market to a high-end gourmet shop. Over time, The Smokehouse Market has kept its focus on the smoked meats and sausages that have made its reputation for the past eighty-plus years. Sandwiched between its deli/sandwich counter and fresh meat cases are shelves and cold cases stocked with domestic and international delights, from cheeses and condiments to fresh-baked pies and locally fried chips.

Pick up a hand-basket and shop while taking advantage of daily samplings of meats, cheeses, and dips, strategically placed on small niche tables along the narrow aisles. I love sampling. It inspires me to fill that basket and helps me decide what sandwich or salad to order from the deli. It's reason to walk a little slower to better survey the fresh meat and seafood case, where the smoked jumbo shrimp and the heritage hog chops wait.

Shopping can make one thirsty. Satisfy that thirst with wine. The Smokehouse has more than one hundred labels, the most popular selected from the thousand-label wine list next door at Annie Gunn's, the Smokehouse's sister eatery.

16806 Chesterfield Airport Rd., Chesterfield
636-532-3314
anniegunns.com

Photo credit: (top, both) Suzanne Corbett; (bottom, both) The Smokehouse Market

PAUL'S MARKET

For nearly sixty years, Paul's Market in Ferguson has been known as "the biggest little steak store in St. Louis," a place where you can always find the holy grail of steaks—USDA Prime. Those prime steaks, along with chops and other fresh meats, are hand selected and cut to order. That's a big deal; most other meat shops cut and prepackage their steaks, forcing customers to take what they have or leave it.

Gary Crump, Paul's son and a second-generation butcher/grocer, follows his dad's commitment to continue and maintain an old-fashioned butcher shop atmosphere that emphasizes customer service. If you're looking for something special and don't see it in the case, ask. Or if you need your steak or chops custom cut, they'll do it. That's what old-fashioned butcher shops did and what Paul's still does.

While Paul's butcher and deli counter is the centerpiece of the business, you'll want to shop the shelves. The grocery section might be small, but it's mighty. Look for homegrown produce in season and locally produced items such as pickles, sauces, breads, and roasted coffees. Many of those items are featured in the shop's hot lunch and dinner specials, which consist of smoked barbecue meats, burgers, and salads—good for a fast lunch or supper in the parking lot.

1020 N Elizabeth Ave., Ferguson
314-524-3652
paulsmarketstl.com

Photo credit: Paul's Market

To get the best deals it pays to stay connected. Keep in the loop with Paul's online newsletter and e-blasts announcing its weekly Butcher Block specials.

JAY INTERNATIONAL FOODS

When I taught Asian cooking classes back in the day, wonton wrappers and ginger root were far from mainstream. That's how I found specialty grocers like Jay Asia on South Grand. I still find basic egg roll supplies there, along with more exotic ingredients such as lemon grass, Thai eggplants, and lime leaves.

Jay Asia became Jay International to better serve St. Louis's multinational culinary communities, which hail from Europe, Asia, Africa, and the Middle East, along with the Americas. Its global inventory brings tastes from many homelands, and both the casual food curious and the hardcore foodie will find an adventure among its crowded shelves.

Follow your nose to find interesting aromas. I don't necessarily mean bad smells, just unfamiliar, like the hundreds of bottles, jars, and canned goods only identifiable by label illustrations or attached translations. It's a fun situation that adds to the Jay shopping mystique, as well as an opportunity to interact with fellow customers who can help you figure out what an item is or how it's cooked.

To locate the global ingredients, you need to follow the international flags that hang over the aisles. They serve as your roadmap to find that bottle of Thai fish sauce or jar of German sweet-sour red cabbage and everything else in between.

3172 S Grand Blvd., St. Louis
314-772-2552
facebook.com/JayInternationalFoods

Photo credit: Jay International Foods

If you never shopped Jay's plan to spend some time. You'll need lots of time to survey the thousands of bottles and jars alone—discovering varieties of soy sauce you ever knew existed.

SOULARD
FARMERS MARKET

Soulard Market is St. Louis's oldest continuously running farm market. Its history stretches from St. Louis's earliest days—promoted as being established in 1779, when it was just a stop on the trail between colonial St. Louis and its southern neighbor Carondelet, which is now part of the city limits.

Soulard Market, which occupies two city blocks, is named for its benefactor, Julia Soulard, who deeded the land to St. Louis in 1841. Its design combines covered open-air stalls that shoot off as wings from the main market house's grand hall. The grand hall building allows the market to remain open year-round, Wednesdays through Saturdays. Inside the market house is a collection of shops: a flower shop, a spice shop, Frandeka Meat Market, and a bakery. Many of these shops, like Frandeka and area farm vendors, have sold in the market for generations.

The best time for produce is April through October, when the area farmers fill the stalls with local produce and products. As the summer fades to fall, the products change. In May you'll find strawberries, while hot peppers and tomatoes will appear from July through early September. Expect pumpkins and sweet potatoes in October. Look for Soulard's specialty vendors, from the Amish who sell homemade jams and pickles to poultry men with live chickens and brown eggs, reportedly the best for Sunday omelets.

730 Carroll St., St. Louis
314-622-4180
soulardmarket.com

Photo credit: (top) Soulard Farmer Market; (bottom, both) Suzanne Corbett

STUCKMEYER'S FARM MARKET AND GREENHOUSE

I was raised on a south St. Louis County truck farm. So were the Stuckmeyers, fourth-generation farmers who operate Stuckmeyer's Farm Market and Greenhouse, located just over the St. Louis County line in Fenton, off Highway 141.

Stuckmeyer's, the market, sits on the edge of its fields of row crops. The farmstead itself could be called retro farming, but I prefer to call it traditional. This is planting and farming using traditional methods handed down by those early southside St. Louis German gardeners who made their living raising and selling seasonal vegetables and small fruits. It's a proud tradition that hasn't changed at Stuckmeyer's, which has been a popular farm market for decades— long before the farm-to-fork movement made family farms trendy.

The secret to shopping farm markets is knowing what's in season. To check what's ripe, or as we used to say, "what was coming on," look inside Stuckmeyer's red barn market to get your share of the latest pick. Tomatoes, bell peppers, corn, and cucumbers are expected from July to September. Check the small signs stuck in the ground along the road advertising such seasonal delights as blackberries and peaches. For pumpkins, squash, gourds, and mums, visit in fall, when you can catch Stuckmeyer's Halloween Farm Fun Days, held every weekend in October.

249 Schneider Dr., Fenton
636-349-1225
stuckmeyers.com

Photo credit: Suzanne Corbett

ECKERT'S COUNTRY STORE & FARMS

Farm-fresh produce, entertainment, and general all-around good eating is the trifecta that has made Eckert's a winner. It's a family farm whose efforts helped pioneer the idea of agritourism, a concept originally designed to help keep family farms going. As a result, Eckert's Illinois farms are a favored destination, an easy drive within thirty minutes of the Gateway Arch.

The farm experience is what drives agritourism—tempting folks to pick their own peaches, berries, and apples. I prefer to let others work the fields, opting instead to stroll the farm market to pick up a prepacked peck of peaches or apples. The market house is where you'll find gardening workshops scheduled throughout the year, designed to help frustrated backyard or patio gardeners grow a better crop.

A few years back, Eckert's expanded its Belleville location, which now incudes the farm and orchard headquarters, a bigger country store, a garden shop, and a restaurant. Beyond the produce bins there's a now a bakery, where Belleville's famous peanut squares are baked, and an extensive meat and cheese counter featuring locally processed products. The best farm addition to its crowded event calendar is its cooking classes, held in its new kitchen classroom. Classes feature themes and recipes spotlighting seasonal crops, including Eckert's signature peaches and apples.

951 S Green Mount Rd., Belleville, IL
618-233-0513
eckerts.com

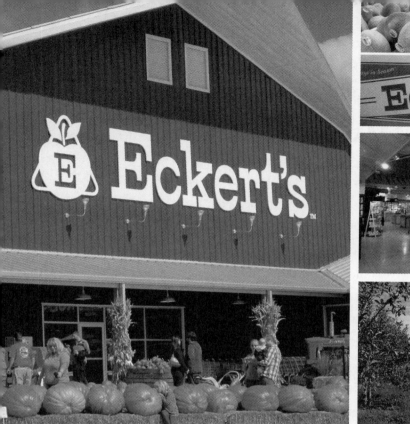

Photo credit: Eckert's Country Store & Farms; box of peaches, Suzanne Corbett

Creating memories drives Eckert's monthly special events, which are staged around thier signature crops of apples, peaches, and berries. Don't miss apple knocking–apple picking and riding the orchard tram during the fall.

THIES FARM AND GREENHOUSES

Few family farms have survived, especially those from the nineteenth century. As the saying goes, "it's a hard row to hoe." Farming is a tough way to make a living and many family farms haven't lasted. That's not the case for Thies Farm and Greenhouses, which has survived and thrived since 1885. Their original North County farmstead near Interstate 70 is still open for business, in addition to its Maryland Heights farm market, nestled in the middle of vast fields along the Missouri River bottoms.

To visit Thies Farm in Maryland Heights, follow the gravel drive off the outer road to the market barn complex. You'll likely pass workers picking and cultivating the fields. On weekends, fields are filled with families picking the seasonal U-pick crop. I prefer picking my vegetables from those displayed in bushel baskets and trays at the market stand, where I can buy any quantity I need, from a single tomato to a bushel of cucumbers. Not into canning or pickling? Fuhgeddaboudit. Thies Farm stocks an extensive selection of homemade jams, jellies, pickles, and salsas made from its local crops. To explore Thies Farm, begin by asking what's ripe, then plan your menu accordingly, based on the fresh pick of the day.

14101 Creve Coeur Mill Rd., Maryland Heights
314-469-7559
thiesfarm.com

Photo credit: (top and left) Suzanne Corbett; (bottom right) Thies Farm and Greenhouses

DIGREGORIO'S MARKET

Shopping and eating my way through Sicily is my passion. It doesn't matter that I've never been to Sicily. I don't have to. I live in St. Louis, where I can go to The Hill and get the best Sicilian-style groceries, meats, and cheeses anytime I want.

The Hill, named such because it was one of the highest points in the city, was established by Italian immigrants, mostly Sicilian, who came to St. Louis in the late nineteenth century. It became the epicenter for St. Louis's Italian-American culture, whose community reputation forged its now-famous grocery stores, meat shops, and eateries. DiGregorio's is counted among The Hill's largest, most successful specialty grocers.

DiGregorio's is a one-stop shop for Italian wines, specialty meats, sausages, and cheeses, along with an ever-growing list of authentic ingredients that fill shelves with products ranging from imported pastas and olive oils to cannoli shells and roasted coffees.

One of DiGregorio's market standouts is its own fresh housemade salsiccia—that's Italian sausage spiced either hot or mild. Italian dinners made easy are found in the freezer case, where frozen entrees—the meatballs, chicken spiedini, and braciole, the delectable Sicilian rolled beef stuffed with breadcrumbs, cheese, and salami, are the top picks, all authentically produced with St. Louis Italian pride.

5200 Daggett Ave., St. Louis
314-776-1062
digregoriofoods.com

Photo credit: Suzanne Corbett

SMOKED, CURED, AND SAUCED

VOLPI FOODS

Why buy imported when you can buy the best artisan Italian meats on The Hill? Salame, coppa, sopressa, mortadella, and prosciutto await.

5258 Daggett Ave., St. Louis
314-446-7950, volpifoods.com

Photo credit: Volpi Foods

DALIE'S SMOKEHOUSE

Placing an order at Dalie's Smokehouse begins with checking the menu—that is, the sold-out menu hanging near the register.

I'm not the only one who has stepped inside and stopped dead in their tracks to stare, hoping that what I'm craving hasn't sold out. Sad if it is, but no worries! There are plenty of choices, including those off-menu specials written on paper scraps taped helter-skelter under the menu board. It's a cool, quirky little touch, reminiscent of the days when barbecue restaurants were proudly called joints.

This throwback feel extends to the barbecue itself, which takes on a West Memphis, Arkansas, accent. It's the style Dalie's co-owner Skip Steele learned from his grandpa, "Papa Joe" Dalie Wells, a style defined by sweet wood smoke and spice rubs, with its sauce on the side. Those sauces come corralled like beer in a six-pack, packed in squeeze bottles featuring everything from the sweet and tangy Papa Joe's Original and smoky Sweet Hope to those that delightfully zap the taste buds, like the sweet and fiery Voodoo and the defiantly different Cranberry Cayenne.

Squeeze that sauce and use it as a standalone flavor, or mix them together to enhance the smoked meats or the sides. Otherwise, just go au naturale and hold the sauce.

2951 Dougherty Ferry Rd., St. Louis
636-529-1898
daliessmokehouse.com

Photo credit: Dalie's Smokehouse

Forget spiral sliced, sugar encrusted hams during the holidays. Dalie's has an alternative, a house cured, smoked ham covered and baked with a bacon lattice blanket. As a reference, it's the same ham used to make Dalie's Cuban sandwiches.

PAPPY'S SMOKEHOUSE

When a barbecue joint posts its hours as "Open till we sell out," it's a good sign. Pappy's Smokehouse is such a place. It's the place where Mike Emerson, Pappy's co-founder, struck a match that helped ignite the flames of St. Louis's barbecue culture and helped earn St. Louis a designation on the Barbecue Triangle (St. Louis, Memphis, and Kansas City).

Pappy's pitmasters, aka the hog whisperers, tend the smokers daily. Each is stacked with spice-rubbed rib racks and pork shoulders. Sharing smoker space with the pork are chicken, turkey breast, and beef brisket, all of which are smoked over sweet apple and cherry wood. When you bite into the meat, look for the smoke ring. That's the dark red or deep pink color line that appears in the meat during the smoking process, a process that's achieved through low and slow smoking. That ring is the visible sign barbecue judges look for to evaluate quality.

While Pappy's smokes slow, its service is fast. Order up and don't be afraid to try the Hot Link Frito Pie, a layered mix of Fritos, baked beans, smoked hot links, red onions, shredded cheddar, and sour cream. Consider it the pitmaster's interpretation of the Slinger.

3106 Olive St., St. Louis
314-535-4340
pappyssmokehouse.com

Photo credit: Pappy's Smokehouse

SUGARFIRE SMOKE HOUSE

Fire spreads fast. It's a fact, especially at Sugarfire. Since 2012, its operations have spread to six locations throughout three St. Louis-area counties. Its success is a testament to its pitmaster/partner Mike Johnson, who has given his signature smoked meats a twist through inspired combinations that kick the flavor up a notch. That's no surprise, considering Johnson worked for Emeril Lagasse and at a fancy restaurant in France before earning the title "pitmaster" from four-time World Champion Pitmaster Myron Mixon.

At Sugarfire, expect conventional barbecue mixed with the unconventional. Look beyond the standard rubbed and smoked ribs, pulled pork, and brisket. For instance, brisket surfaces in a smoked brisket cheesesteak sandwich. The chicken biscuit, a southern delight, has been given the good-old-boy gourmet treatment by marinating boneless chicken thighs in a combination of buttermilk, pickle juice, and "nunya"—that's short for "none of your business." Next it gets smoked, breaded, fried, and drenched with hot sauce, slapped on a biscuit, and slathered with honey butter.

Gild your barbecue by adding the housemade pimento cheese to any sandwich. Or eat a little lower on the food chain and indulge with the smoked portobello or smoked fried artichokes with a lemon aioli. This is food that earns Sugarfire the title I'll call "barbecue chic."

9200 Olive Blvd. (original location), St. Louis
314-997-2301
sugarfiresmokehouse.com

Photo credit: (top and left) Suzanne Corbett; (right) Sugarfire Smoke House

CAFÉ TELEGRAPH

Once upon a time, St. Louis barbecue was made on brick barbecue pits, custom built, complete with a chimney. These were monster pits the size of bungalows built in backyards by those related to brick masons and by parks departments to accommodate community summer throwdowns. They were great and produced a nicely charred and subtle smokiness I find at Café Telegraph, where the smoke shack provides pork steaks large enough to literally cover the plate. The pork steaks, thick cut and weighing in at two pounds, are Café Telegraph's claim to fame. They're a St. Louis culinary icon that's sweetly rubbed and smoked, and which I cover in sauce. Egad, that's a crime in hardcore barbecue circles, but I like it anyway! Most St. Louisans do. That's the reason we use more sauce that anywhere else in the country.

Telegraph Café's other bodacious offerings include thick-sliced meatloaf and meaty slabs of ribs. For the non-red-meat eater, there are smoked and blackened salmon and brined and smoked half-chickens and wings. If you like your wings crisp, let them take a dip in the deep fryer. Finally, there's Stan's Big Bomber, a 20-ounce mountain of pulled pork piled on Texas toast with slaw and bacon, served with a side. Find a friend and share it or come hungry—occasionally the Big Bomber is devoured by one.

2650 Telegraph Rd., St. Louis
314-200-9952
cafetelegraph.com

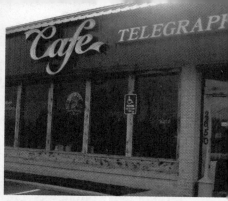

Photo credit: (left, top right) Suzanne Corbett; (bottom right) Café Telegraph

Beyond the barbecue take time to drink in the décor highlighting Jefferson Barracks Park's military history. It may inspire you to take a drive after dinner through historic JB, which is a five-minute drive away.

PICK-A-BONE

At a time when pop-up food venues are all the rage, roadside barbecue stands have become a rarity. That's unless you're traveling down Highway 141 near the Highway 21 interchange, where Pick-A-Bone BBQ pitches its tent year-round next to the legendary roadside Pink Elephant at the Gas 'n' Stuff parking lot. Under the tent, you'll find a doublewide, charcoal-fueled, ironclad barbecue operated by pitmasters Marion and Jody Brown. The specialties: full-cut spareribs, thick-cut pork steaks, pulled pork, and chicken.

Pick-A-Bone's pop-up menu is simple—nothing fancy or pretentious, just retro barbecue like it used to be, served with sides of beans, slaw, and potato salad that's better than grandma's. Just don't tell her. Everything is wrapped to carry home. Or if you're hungry and can't wait, eat onsite at one of the nearby picnic tables.

Rib slabs, smoked pork, chicken, and the occasional beef ribs appear on the menu along with thick-sliced and sauced pork steaks, white chili, and hot dogs, all designed as grab-and-go dinners and sandwiches. To decide what to pick at Pick-A-Bone, do as one loyal customer suggested and throw a dart at the menu—it will always hit something good.

2599 Highway 141, Fenton
314-724-7631

Photo credit: (top left; bottom, both) Suzanne Corbett; (top right) Jim Corbett III

PIEKUTOWSKI'S EUROPEAN STYLE SAUSAGE

There's a good reason Piekutowski's Polish-style sausages were blessed as a must-have by Pope John Paul II, who craved them during his 1999 St. Louis visit. The reason? These sausages are the real deal, authentically made just like they were in the old country by the Piekutowski family. The tradition continues using the same recipes and sausage-making techniques that the Piekutowskis have been using for nearly eight decades at their northside sausage shop, where mountains of seasoned kielbasa (Polish sausage links) have been made and sold. Some of those made their way into my mother's kitchen, where they were steamed with barrel kraut and potatoes as a quick supper—a recipe I can still recommend.

The spicier hot links version of kielbasa, laced with garlic, pepper, and cayenne, is one of the European sausage varieties produced on site. Krakow, a coarse-cut smoked sausage that's a distant cousin to salami, is a Polish specialty, as is Piekutowski's German beer salami. Beer isn't in the sausage mix, but when it's made into a sandwich, it's the perfect foil for a beer. Be sure to save a beer to have with another sandwich stuffed with Old Country bologna, a totally different taste and texture that you'll never confuse with Oscar Mayer.

4100 N Florissant Ave., St. Louis
314-534-6256
piekutowskis.com

Photo credit: Piekutowski's

ST. LOUIS HOME FIRES

St. Louis Homes Fires is known as a pitmaster's hookup for new pits and smokers and a one-stop shop for backyard barbecue chefs and those barbecue aficionados who search for sauces and rubs. Think of it as "rub and sauce central." No offense, Maull's or Lawry's seasoned salt, for which I still hold sentimental affection, but today's barbecue fans crave more. I'm talking about upscale, downhome, knocking-it-out-of-the-park sauces and rubs that competition pitmasters use. And that's exactly what lines the walls at St. Louis Home Fires, which, by the way, is the home of the St. Louis BBQ Society.

Peruse the shelves and you'll find what you're looking for—from sweet and smoky sauces and vinegar mops to killer fiery hot sauces. There are plenty of unique choices, including those with limited distribution such as Bone Suckin' Mustard Sauce and Twisted Melon Madness, which contains watermelon. Rub and spice choices include brine mixes and spice injection blends, with eye-catching names like Butcher BBQ Prime Dust and Code Three, a rub collection that's become a first-responder fundraiser. If you smoke, grab a sack of aromatic smoking wood chips and try one of the more unusual woods, such as grapevine or mulberry.

15053 Manchester Rd., Ballwin
636-256-6564
stlouishomefires.com

Photo credit: St. Louis Home Fires

Looking for tips on how to make a better backyard barbecue? This is the place where novices and professional pit masters gather to get the latest on equipment, trends, and techniques. If you have a barbecue/grilling question you can get it answered here.

URBAN CHESTNUT BREWING COMPANY (page 40)

CARL'S DRIVE INN (page 184)

ANHEUSER~BUSCH (page 37)

DALIE'S SMOKEHOUSE (page 102)

PHO GRAND (page 54)

BALABAN'S (page 52)

AL'S RESTAURANT (page 72)

RIGAZZI'S (page 156)

SUGARFIRE SMOKE HOUSE (page 106)

BONES FRENCH QUARTER (page 190)

CLEMENTINE'S NAUGHTY AND NICE CREAMERY (page 144)

HODAK'S RESTAURANT & BAR (page 176)

THE FOUNTAIN ON LOCUST (page 146)

CEDAR LAKE CELLARS (page 36)

SUMP COFFEE (page 48)

BIG CHIEF (page 84)

GROWN CANDY KITCHEN (page 80)

G & W SAUSAGE

Ask a German sausage maker to name the brat variety he likes best, and he'll likely tell you "all of them." I can agree—particularly if I'm washing that brat down with a beer. Perhaps the only thing better than shopping for brats at G & W is drinking a beer, which is exactly what's offered to interested customers of legal age. Granted, the cold beer is good, but the best at G & W is the wurst. Sausages are made using family recipes brought from Bavaria, resulting in the largest selection of authentic Bavarian-style sausages in the region.

Topping G & W's wurst roster is the original bratwurst known as the Grant's Farm brat, the brat of choice served at the farm for more than forty years. From the brat, G & W tweaks the recipe to create garlic brats, beer brats, and bacon and cheddar with or without jalapeños, along with a few more blends. Beyond the brats is an impressive sausage assortment ranging from Polish hot links and Cajun andouille to German knackwurst and old-fashioned wieners that are still strung together in ropes. German-loving wurst gourmands will revel in the landjäger (smoked sausage sticks) and the rarest of delicacies, the leberkäse and the spicy hausmacher—called pâté by some, but to those who love it, it's simply liverwurst.

4828 Parker Ave., St. Louis
314-352-5066
gwsausage.com

Photo credit: G & W Sausage

HOT HEARTHS, COOL CREAMS

EL CHICO BAKERY

The place for authentic conchas (sweet yeast-raised, sugar-topped bread), empanadas, and tres leches cakes. The weekend must-try specialty is the handmade tamales.

2634 Cherokee St., St. Louis
314-664-2212, facebook.com/ElChicoBakery

Photo credit: Suzanne Corbett

THE BLUE OWL
RESTAURANT AND BAKERY

Itinerant bakers are those who baked and sold their wares at festivals and craft fairs. It's a past I share with Mary Hostetter, who moved beyond home baking to open The Blue Owl, the restaurant and bakery located in the old river town of Kimmswick. Since The Blue Owl's opening, its ovens haven't stopped baking the cookies, cakes, and pies that have made Mary famous.

Once you're inside Kimmswick's tiny city limits, The Blue Owl is easy to find. Just look for the crowd gathered around the front porch and the line waiting to get a table. Luckily, bakery customers don't have to wait in the restaurant line. Just step inside, go to the bakery counter, and get ready to indulge your sweet tooth. All the pastries, cakes, and pies are still made the way Mary originally prepared them, by hand. Handmade, small-batch goodness is the secret behind The Blue Owl's quality, not to mention its signature dessert, the Levee High Caramel Apple Pecan Pie. It starts with a tower of apples made by neatly hand-stacking apples inside the cone-shaped vintage Tupperware salad lettuce bowl that's inverted into the pie pan. It's then baked and draped with a caramel nut coating. No wonder it was one of Oprah's favorite things.

6116 Second St., Kimmswick
636-464-3128
theblueowl.com

Photo credit: (top left) The Blue Owl Restaurant and Bakery; (bottom left, right, both)
Suzanne Corbett

Forget the diet and eat up. Pie is always worth the calories.

SARAH'S CAKE SHOP ON CENTRAL

When Sarah is on the road, she's sometimes hard to find—so keep a look out for Sarah's Cake Shop food truck. Packed onboard is an ever-changing selection of handheld sweets, brownies, cupcakes, cookies, and devilishly decadent chocolate-covered cheesecake bombs.

Finding Sarah's truck depends on if you're social—if you don't tweet, you won't find where she's parked. As a result, you could go hungry, that is, if it weren't for her two brick-and-mortar shops, one in Old Town Eureka on Central Avenue and the other off Clarkson Road in Chesterfield.

Sarah's on Central has of late diversified and now includes a café. However, most hit the door to satisfy sweet cravings. To get the sweet pick you crave, plan to arrive early rather than late, otherwise pickings are slim. Often the day's more popular items—such as the Crooey, the love child of puff pastry and a gooey butter cake, made by fitting puff pastry into a muffin cup topped with gooey butter filling and baking it—sell out. They're on the oh-my-god kind of good list alongside the Glitter Bites, Sarah's signature sweet consisting of featherlight cream-filled cake balls rolled in sanding sugar. Both are well worth breaking any diet for.

127 S Central Ave., Eureka
636-938-4800
sarahscakeshopstl.com

Photo credit: (left) Jim Corbett III; (right, both) Sara's Cake Shop

PICCIONE PASTRY

Think cannolis are exclusive to Italian bakeries on The Hill? Guess again. Cannolis are the main attraction at Piccione's, an Italian-focused bakery perched in the heart of the U-City Loop at Skinker and Delmar Boulevard—an intersection that has quickly become St. Louis's cannoli epicenter. With nearly a quarter-million cannolis sold in its first four years, Piccione's pastry chefs have proved there's more than one way to stuff a cannoli.

Classic cannoli lovers, don't freak out. Piccione's creates the classic original Sicilian cannoli: the thin, crisp, fried pastry shell stuffed with creamy ricotta, whipped cream, and mascarpone. Then there's a lighter version, the Piccione Signature, which lightens the filling with custard. Both versions rock; however, there are more options. To decode which cannoli is which, look at how its ends are finished. If the ends are covered in pistachios, it's a pistachio cannoli; chocolate chips indicate chocolate, and so on. My cannoli craving is satisfied with the Marsala black cherry or whatever the weekly special, dubbed the Crazy Cannoli, might be. I'm waiting for the return of the Bacon Chocolate and Pop Rock cannoli.

Sweet temptations beyond the cannoli include rum-soaked cassata cakes, napoleons, ricotta cheesecakes, and trays upon trays of authentic Italian cookies, featuring rarities like the Italian tricolor, all baked to seduce your sweet tooth and ignite cravings. Cravings are best paired with an espresso.

6197 Delmar St., St. Louis
314-932-1355
piccionepastry.com

Photo credit: Piccione Pastry

FEDERHOFER'S BAKERY

Once upon a time, every neighborhood had a corner bakeshop, sometimes more than one. Bakeshops, especially the St. Louis German bakeries I grew up with, seemed as prevalent as corner taverns. One of the last remaining German bakeshops is Federhofer's, where old-style seed rye shares racks with old-fashioned cream and cobblestone breads. Federhofer's is a place where seekers of the authentic can find classic baked goods seldom found anywhere outside St. Louis bakeshops, including bags of seed horns (crescent-shaped dinner rolls), coconut toast (a homemade Melba toasted with sweet coconut), and freshly made Parker House rolls.

Federhofer's boasts three generations of bakers who bake from Old World family recipes, including instructions for baking original gooey butter cake from a 1930s recipe. Tyler May, the proud third-generation Federhofer's baker, will tell all you home bakers that the original gooey butter recipe doesn't call for cream cheese. To re-create the original, forget those recipes circulating on the internet. Instead, come to Federhofer's, where it's baked in two styles, the original gooey butter cake and the deep gooey butter cake. Deep butter is a sponge-like cake that's sprinkled with powdered sugar. Go for the deep butter along with one more unique find, which few bakers today know about, let along bake—the featherlight chiffon cheesecake.

9005 Gravois Rd., St. Louis
314-832-5116
federhofersbakery.com

142

Photo credit: Federhofer's Bakery

CLEMENTINE'S NAUGHTY AND NICE CREAMERY

Naughty and nice collectively make for good at Clementine's, a microcreamery that has made its reputation making ice creams flavored with liquor (the naughty) and without (the nice). Haven't heard of microcreamery ice cream? It's defined as small-batch, handcrafted, all-natural ice cream with a low overrun, meaning it's not pumped up with air. It also has to have sixteen percent butterfat. Regular store brands have about ten percent. Taking it one step further, Clementine's owner, Tamara Keefe, can even tell you about the farm and the cows that produce the milk for her creams.

Making the nice, non-boozy flavor list are the award-winning Gooey Butter Cake, Madagascar Vanilla, and Kickass Chocolate, not to mention wilder combinations like the Manchego Truffle Honey and Lemongrass Coconut. As a whiskey girl, I'm attracted to the boozy, naughty selections like the Bourbon Kentucky Pie. Wait, I like rum too, so I can't pass up the Boozy Banana Rum swirled with Salted Butterscotch Caramel or a dish of the seasonal Caribbean Cool, a cocktail mix of Malibu rum, OJ, cranberry juice, peach schnapps, and vodka. If you're a wine drinker, then try the Chocolate Cabernet. These are all sinfully created flavors that could have tempted Carrie Nation, the hatchet-wielding temperance leader, to jump off the wagon and imbibe.

1637 S 18th St. (the original scoop shop), St. Louis
314-858-6100
clementinescreamery.com

144

Photo credit: Clementine's Naughty and Nice Creamery

THE FOUNTAIN ON LOCUST

Black and white tile floors, wood bars, and Art Deco murals set the mood to have an ice cream soda at The Fountain on Locust. Make that a house specialty retro ice cream soda, float, or cocktail, many of which are named for vintage autos in honor of The Fountain on Locust's original occupant, the Supreme Car Company. The 1916 showroom is where Stutz automobiles were the main attraction. Although the showroom is now the dining room, Stutz still is a luxury indulgence, served either as a customized sundae or as the deluxe Stutz Bearcat, a combo of sliced bananas, hot fudge, hot caramel, butter pecan ice cream, and whipped cream.

The on-duty soda jerk gladly mixes eggs creams, soda floats, and malts in addition to an impressive list of retro cocktails, including the nearly forgotten knickerbocker and high ball. And oh yes, did I say martinis? Ice cream martinis??? There are twenty-five different boozy martini concoctions, which have become the Fountain's claim to fame. Liquor is a key ingredient in the Fountain's adult ice cream sauces while champagne appears in cocktails and Guinness is used to create ice cream floats.

Once you get beyond the adult cocktails, the handmade whipped cream, and the sauces and toppings, there's the Fountain's ice cream, which is produced and aged at a Wisconsin family dairy. Aging ice cream allows it to develop a smoother, more complex flavor profile. The Fountain is the only place in St. Louis featuring aged ice cream.

3037 Locust St., St. Louis
314-535-7800
fountainonlocust.com

Photo credit: The Fountain on Locust

Ask for a west side booth where guests can listen to the only Restaurant Radio Comedy Serial, Soup Hospital. Every two minutes a new episode is aired.

ICES PLAIN & FANCY

Ices Plain & Fancy isn't your run-of-the-mill ice cream shop. Ice cream here is made to order and flash-churned using liquid nitrogen, a technique that delivers culinary theatrics via cold smoke clouds and blowtorches. It sounds new but it's not—it's a 19th-century technology invented by Agnes Marshall, author of *Ices Plain and Fancy* (the store's namesake) and holder of the 1894 patent for an ice cream maker using "liquid air," aka liquid nitrogen. The effect then, as it is now, is an incredible show to watch, with a finale you get to eat.

The show begins with picking a flavor. The mix is then placed in a spinning mixer and nitrogen is added. It flash freezes at –321° in less than a minute, all while smoke rolls out of the mixing bowl. A blowtorch is used to heat the bowl to unstick the frozen cream. It's a great show, but one has to wonder, why bother? Here's why: flash nitro freezing forms tiny ice crystals in the ice cream, resulting in a silky smooth and dense texture that traditional churning can't produce. A word of caution in regard to the liquor-flavored ice creams—nitrogen freezes alcohol as fast as the cream, so the proof remains the same as in a regular cocktail, making those creams and ices only for clientele 21 and older.

2256 S 39th St., St. Louis
314-601-3604
icesplainandfancy.com

Photo credit: (bottom left) Suzanne Corbett; (others) Ices Plain & Fancy

FRITZ'S FROZEN CUSTARD

Some things are better left the old way, and frozen custard is one of them. That's the sentiment of Fritz's Frozen Custard fans, who are quick to instruct the uninformed about the difference between ice cream and frozen custard. That difference is the recipe. Frozen custard typically has egg yolks, but not so at Fritz's, where the recipe is made in the French vanilla style using egg whites, making it lower in cholesterol and also lower in fat. Try the no-sugar-added version for another option that's a win-win for anyone looking for a healthier alternative to traditional ice cream.

Another difference—real frozen custard is always churned and hand-dipped, allowing it to transform easily into treats such as concretes, shakes, and gourmet sundaes, especially Fritz's signature Turtle Sundae. A favorite for more than thirty years, the Turtle is topped with homemade hot fudge and caramel sauces and finished with custom-roasted, lightly salted pecans.

Standard vanilla and chocolate flavors are available every day along with daily and seasonal flavors. To get the latest flavor updates, check the online calendar or sign up for tweets. I stay connected to the West County location via Facebook throughout the season, which runs from March to November.

815 Meramec Station Rd., Valley Park
636-225-8737
facebook.com/FritzsWestCo

Photo credit: (left) Suznne Corbett; (center, right) Frit's Frozen Custard

ST. LOUIS ITALIAN

ADRIANA'S ON THE HILL

Fast, affordable, and hearty is the winning trifecta at Adriana's, known for well-stuffed sandwiches, pizza, salads, and pasta. Lunch hours only, so don't be late to queue up and place your order for dine-in or carryout.

5101 Shaw Ave., St. Louis
314-773-3833, adrianasonthehill.com

Photo credit: Adriana's

LORUSSO'S CUCINA

"We're not your usual Italian." That has been Rich LoRusso's mantra since opening LoRusso's Cucina more than thirty years ago. It's a claim that still holds true today, thanks to Rich's unique spin on Italian cooking. It's a spin that combines family recipes, popular St. Louis Italian dishes, and creative new gourmet plates with an Italian accent, all of which emphasize authentic ingredients and balanced flavors. It was an unusual take on Italian cuisine at a time when the majority of Italian restaurants were defined by oregano and pastas overloaded with heavy sauce. Not so here, especially when it comes to pasta, the home of the annual LoRusso's Pasta Bowl.

Pasta Bowl invites customers to enter their favorite pasta recipes for the opportunity to have their dish placed on the menu, a temptation even celebrity chef Mario Batali couldn't resist—but didn't win. The 2017 winner was capellini pomodoro, or angel-hair pasta with sun-dried tomatoes, fresh basil, and other herbs in a light sauce of garlic, olive oil, butter, and Parmesan. Pasta lovers are encouraged to order the dish to benefit Operation Food Search, to which LoRusso's donates two dollars for each plate served. To date, nearly $70,000 has been raised from the Pasta Bowl, which equates to a mountain for pasta for an excellent cause.

3121 Watson Rd., St Louis
314-647-6222
lorussos.com

Photo credit: LoRusso's Cucina

Attention all wine and antipasto lovers. Look for LoRusso's Top Shelf Wine Tastings, usually staged monthly, paired with the restaurant's signature Antipasto Buffet.

CHARLIE GITTO'S DOWNTOWN

Before the tsunami of pasta restaurants spread throughout St. Louis, there was Charlie Gitto's Pasta House. Not to be confused with Charlie Sr.'s sons' operations on The Hill, West County, or St. Charles, Charlie Gitto's Downtown is the original, a favored haunt for politicians, businessmen, and baseball players. During Cardinals baseball games, the dining room is a sea of red, filled with fans before and after the game for pasta and Italian specialties, foods that have made Charlie Gitto's a downtown landmark. But don't just take my word for it. Check out the photos covering the walls. It's a who's who of St. Louis and beyond—celebs and regular joes who have eaten at Charlie's.

Beyond the photos, the rustic sports bar décor, and the food, fans come to Gitto's to see Charlie, who still holds court at the bar or the front window table, named for one of Gitto's better-known baseball friends, Tommy Lasorda. Charlie gladly spins tales, talks baseball, and is happy to make menu recommendations—usually baked lasagna, the special Gitto's Italian Salad, and a cold beer.

207 N Sixth St., St. Louis
314-436-2828
charliegittosdt.com

Photo credit: Charlie Gitto's

Toasted Ravioli. Enough said.

RIGAZZI'S

Restaurants often promote a signature drink, but not at Rigazzi's. It has a signature glass, the Frozen Fishbowl—a chilled goblet, which in the 1890s was called a nickel beer and was served with a free lunch. Well, times have changed. No more free lunch, and beer is more than a nickel; however, lunch and dinner at Rigazzi's are worth every nickel, as is the Fishbowl, which holds thirty-two ounces of beer or anything else you want to put in it.

Rigazzi's, opened in 1957 by two buddies, Lou Aiazzi and John Riganti, is considered the oldest operating restaurant on The Hill. They christened the eatery by merging their last names and created a menu that always reflected the Aiazzis' Northern Italian roots along with a blend of American dishes such as fried chicken and open roast beef sandwiches. It's a menu that has worked, with a little bit of something for everyone, and has kept the customers rolling in for its lunch and dinner specials.

Rigazzi's specials and affordable pricing, combined with consistently good Italian fare, has made the restaurant popular from the beginning, drawing nightly crowds. Its success was made famous when the late native of The Hill Yogi Berra said, "It's so crowded nobody goes there anymore." It's been said that Yogi was referring to Rigazzi's.

4945 Daggett Ave., St. Louis
314-772-4900
rigazzis.com

Photo credit: Rigazzi's

Can't make happy hour because you work the overnight shift? No worries. Rigazzi's hosts an early morning happy hour from 8 – 10 a.m.

MASSA'S OF COURSE!

I describe St. Louis Italian-style cuisine as skewed Old World cuisine. A little Sicilian, a little Northern Italian, which local chefs have tweaked to create iconic local dishes such as Massa's Chicken Bianca, a boneless breaded chicken breast. It made its debut in 1976 draped in a white wine mushroom sauce. Massa's is an excellent example of St. Louis Italian cuisine; the plates are generously sauced and cheese is freely used, from mozzarella and provolone to Parmesan and Provel. Yep, Provel, St. Louis's contribution to cheeseography and the quintessential topping on St. Louis thin crust pizza—good stuff for fans who love St. Louis Italian recipes. Jack and Bill Massa helped define these dishes decades ago at their original Massa's location in north St. Louis County.

Today Massa's restaurants number five locations, including my favorite, in Ballwin, which hasn't changed much since the 1980s. Inside, the lighting is subtle and the action at the bar revolves around the barkeep's personality. The menu is rich in pasta, pizza, and entrees cooked with an Italian accent, and tabletop menu cards tout the weekly specials. It's a relaxed place that compels guests to relish the food and conversation. So turn off the cell, pretend its 1989, and enjoy.

15310 Manchester Rd., Ellisville
636-391-3700
stlmassas.com

Photo credit: Suzanne Corbett

AMIGHETTI'S BAKERY & CAFÉ ON THE HILL

One might ask, where's the bread? Doesn't the sign say "bakery"? Indeed, it was just a bakery when Louis Amighetti opened his store in 1921. For the record book, Amighetti's still bakes and sells bread daily, however, most of the bread baked is for sandwiches, the foundation of the famed Amighetti Special, the original St. Louis Hill sandwich that in past years has been crowned Best Roast Beef in the City by Riverfront Times readers. Wait . . . if the term "bakery" had you scratching your head as the main descriptor, calling the Amighetti Special a roast beef sandwich does it injustice. It's so much more—beef, ham, Genoa salami, cheese, lettuce, tomato, pickle, onion, pepperoncini, and a drizzle of sauce take this bad boy to sub status.

Since the sandwich trade eclipsed the bakery in the late 1960s, the business has remained a counter-service operation, focused on the quick-serve and the grab-and-go lunch. While it's not the only sandwich shop on The Hill, it was one of the first, which helped draw non-Italians to The Hill years before culinary destinations were fashionable.

5141 Wilson Ave., St. Louis
314-776-2855
amighettis.com/original-the-hill

THE ITALIAN IMMIGRANTS

Sandwiches   Half $4⁹⁵ Whole $8⁹⁵

Amighetti's Special   Little Bit of Italy
, Genoa Salami, Roast Beef, Brick   Served hot with our own Garlic Butter,
se, Lettuce, Tomato, Pickle, Onion,   Genoa Salami, two blends of Cheese,
ncini, and our own Special Dressing   Onions, and Black Olives

Other Sandwich Favorites
Turkey Delight • Ham & Cheese • Salami & Cheese • Turkey
st Beef • Veggie •   • Egg Salad • Tuna Salad • Chicken Salad
eatball • Roast Beef and Gravy • French Dip •
se/slice $.40   Add meat/slice $.65 Extra sauce on the side $.30

Photo credit: Amighetti's Bakery and Café

There's more to Amighetti's than sandwiches. Pastas, soup, and salads take up over half the menu. Mix it up and partner a pasta or salad with that sandwich order.

THE MISSOURI BAKING COMPANY

It's been nearly a hundred years since the brothers Gambaro (Stephano, Luigi, and Giuseppe) opened their corner bakery, The Missouri Baking Company, on The Hill. They originally opened the business as a commercial operation, baking bread for local restaurants. It was a good idea—however, the brothers didn't consider how the smell of fresh baking bread would seduce the neighbors, bringing them to their doors in search of loaves and sweet treats.

Customers still beat a path to The Missouri Baking Company's door and happily take a number and wait their turn for a chance at the day's fresh bake. Arrive earlier rather than later in the day for the best selection of breads, including the Italian-style loaf, which sells out fast. Another quick sell is the French bread, split and slathered with garlic butter.

I must admit that bread is a second thought when peering at the sweets, Italian pastries, cookies, and cakes. Old-fashioned display cases are lined with trays of cannolis, tiramisu, cookies, and pastries everyday. Look for seasonal finds such as cuccidati (fig- and pine nut-filled cookies), panettone, and cassata cakes layered with sweetened ricotta filling and studded with chocolate chips. Oh yes, and don't miss the chocolate drops, rounds of pound cake covered in dark chocolate icing, which I call the Italian equivalent of a Whoopie Pie.

2027 Edwards St., St. Louis
314-773-6566
facebook.com/The-Missouri-Baking-Company-304406429586958

Photo credit: The Missouri Baking Company

GELATO DI RISO

Attention, ice cream fans yearning for a healthier frozen treat! Your prayers have been answered, thanks to the Italians, the inventors of gelato. Gelato, a cousin to ice cream and frozen custard, is low in fat. It's based on two-percent milk, or even water, when it's used for fruit-based frutta gelatos that are similar to sorbets. To get gelato to the right consistency, Gelato Di Riso creates its slate of flavors using an imported Italian gelato machine, which allows gelato to be done right. It cooks the mix before it churns it into a velvety texture with intense flavors that by all rights should be a diet buster. Instead, gelato is pretty much a guiltless indulgence.

Sinfully good and better for the waistline, gelato has made Gelato Di Riso one of the kings of The Hill, where it produces its gelato for its shop's walk-in trade and for the commercial market, supplying a select group of restaurants and diverse specialty grocery shops from Global Foods in Kirkwood to Neiman Marcus's Zodiac Room. I prefer getting my gelato fix at their Hill location, where I can shop almost anytime except for January and February, when they close for the season.

5204 Wilson Ave., St. Louis
314-664-8488
gelatodiriso.com

Photo credit: Gelato Di Riso

Life is uncertain, eat dessert first. Gelato Di Riso is open 8 a.m. to 9 p.m. so go ahead and eat gelato first for breakfast, lunch, or dinner.

ERIO'S RISTORANTE

Great eateries are often found in unexpected places. Such is the case with Erio's Ristorante, which is tucked in an unassuming strip center that can be easily overlooked—even by my GPS.

But don't give up! Keep looking, because the Sicilian cuisine here has only a slight St. Louis influence. It's a complete one-eighty on the expected St. Louis Italian food, which Pete Pulizzi achieved using recipes from his native Sicily, where he learned the art de cuisine from his mother.

The menu features foods Pulizzi grew up eating, like capellini alla Marissa. Dishes are bright and uncomplicated, allowing the freshness of the ingredients to shine. It's a philosophy Pulizzi has employed from his earliest years as a restaurateur in Florissant, where he perfected his own style of hand-tossed pizza, topped with either mozzarella or Provel. Pizza has become a house favorite at Erio's, along with the manicotti and cannelloni.

Erio's specialties extend well beyond pasta and pizza, though, with 14 different entrée considerations, including bistecca alla Siciliana, a chargrilled strip steak turned in seasoned crumbs and served with a tomato, olive oil, and garlic dipping sauce. Other signature dishes at Erio's are veal scallopini, chicken Marsala, and shrimp scampi. These menu selections prove that good Italian cuisine does exist off The Hill.

951 Jungermann Rd., St. Peters
636-928-0112
eriosristorante.com

YARD BIRD DINNERS

LEMMON'S BY GRBIC

Lemmon's famous chicken has been given a facelift by the Grbic family and has been included on the menu at the resurrected southside eatery that made a reputation on fried chicken and steaks. The new Lemmon's recipe isn't exactly the same, but it's close enough, promising comfort to those seeking a chicken fix.

5800 Gravois Ave., St. Louis,
314-899-9898, lemmonsrestaurant.com

Photo credit: Suzanne Corbett

SOUTHERN

Few foods are more Southern than fried chicken. Deep-fat or pan-fried in vintage cast iron skillets, southern fried chicken has few noteworthy variations except for one—Nashville hot fried chicken. We're talking hot, as in chili-pepper hot. It's the claim to fame at Southern, which has steadily fanned the flames for chicken and hot sauce lovers since its 2015 debut.

Southern's creator, James Beard-nominated chef Rick Lewis, recognized that Nashville hot chicken was poised to take off. So he partnered with Pappy's Smokehouse and opened up next door, where, dare I say it, the chicken caught fire.

So what's the deal with hot chicken? It's all about the recipe. Southern marinates, spice rubs, and deep-fries its yard birds before giving them a quick dip in habanero cayenne chili oil. Sound too hot? Relax, you can customize the burn via Southern's six levels of heat.

For the culinarily meek, opt for the Original, which is milder than the Mild, which is hotter than you think. General Tso's, a kitchen favorite, rates the same level of heat as the Mild. Temperatures rise to Medium, described as "pretty damn hot," Hot ("lips will burn, head will sweat"), and Cluckin Hot, which "may burn the next day."

A friendly fire prevention tip: Tame the flames by nibbling on Southern's cool cucumber pickle chips or sprinkle a little sugar in your mouth to put out the fire.

3108 Olive St., St. Louis
314-531-4668
stlsouthern.com

Photo credit: Southern

How hot is hot chicken? Order a chicken wing at each level of heat and decide for yourself.

THE LEMP MANSION RESTAURANT & INN

Sunday chicken dinner at The Lemp Mansion Restaurant is a classic, a time for family and friends to gather, chow down, and catch up. One friend who may suddenly pop in for a visit is Charles Lemp, who has been known to frequent the bar. He doesn't drink much; after all, Charles shot himself dead in the mansion, as did his brother and father years before him. That's the reason dining guests and staff report paranormal activities—activities some guests welcome to their table, while others are just as happy sticking around to take the mansion's haunted history tour.

It's unclear if Lemp's resident ghosts prefer the Sunday chicken dinner or something else. However, over the past forty years, the all-you-can-eat chicken dinners have proved to be a winner with guests. It was the first meal ever served when the mansion opened for business, and it remains the most popular. Pan-fried chicken piled high on platters served with generous bowls of mashed potatoes and gravy, German green beans, corn, cinnamon apples, slaw, biscuits, and such—it's a bounty that could tempt anyone, even from beyond the grave. But don't be frightened away if you're not a fried chicken fan. Lemp's Sunday dinner has ham or roast beef options.

3322 DeMenil Pl., St. Louis
314-664-8024
lempmansion.com

Photo credit: The Lemp Mansion Restaurant & Inn

171

PORTER'S FRIED CHICKEN

Frying chicken isn't difficult, or at least it shouldn't be. The best recipe is always simple—fresh chicken, seasonings, flour, and hot grease—just like grandma would have fixed if she had had a deep fryer like Porter's.

Porter's Fried Chicken originally opened forty-plus years ago as Charlie's Chicken. The place hasn't changed much. The recipe has been reported as a dry and wet batter with buttermilk and spices, a combination that yields a nice, crispy, brown crust that holds up nicely in the fryer while protecting the bird from drying out. If you want the recipe, you're out of luck. It's a secret. No true chicken shack worth crowing about would ever divulge its recipe. That's why you go to Porter's.

Porter's remains one of the few old-time fried chicken and fish joints where chicken always trumps the fish. It's a place where the surroundings are a little worn—no slick displays or fancy interiors like those big-bucket chains— just plain, simple, and straightforward digs selling what you crave. Regulars know to call ahead to avoid the wait. Not me. I like waiting for my chicken to fry. It's part of the Porter's experience, to sit back and smell the chicken fry.

3628 S Big Bend Rd., St. Louis
314-781-2097
porterschicken.com

CHICKEN DINNERS

Regular: mixed pieces of chicken. Special: your choice.

	REGULAR	SPECIAL
2 piece Snack	3.99	4.99
3 piece Dinner	5.49	6.49
4 piece Box	5.99	7.99
3 piece Wing	4.59	
6 piece Wing	7.19	
Fried Liver	6.19	
Fried Gizzards	6.19	
Chicken Tenders Dinner	6.59	

(Above served with mashed potatoes, slaw and roll)

Fried Liver	4.99
Fried Gizzards	4.99
1/2 Livers - 1/2 Gizzards	4.99
Buffalo Wings (roll) Sauce on the side	6.49
Chicken Tenders	5.39

CHICKEN BUCKETS

	REGULAR	SPECIAL
8 piece Bucket	11.49	13.99
10 piece Bucket	12.59	16.99
12 piece Bucket	13.69	18.99
16 piece Bucket	16.99	23.99
20 piece Bucket	20.49	28.99
16 piece Wing Bucket	15.99	
20 piece Wing Bucket	18.49	

FISH DINNERS

Catfish Nuggets	5.99
4 piece Battered Cod	5.79
1 piece Breaded Cod	4.79
2 piece Breaded Cod	5.89
1 piece Jack Salmon	4.99
2 piece Jack Salmon	6.19
1 piece Catfish	5.89
2 piece Catfish	7.49

(Above served with mashed potatoes, slaw and roll)

SHRIMP DINNERS

6 piece Jumbo Shrimp	6.99
8 oz. Mini Shrimp (18-21 Count)	5.49

(Above served with mashed potatoes, slaw and roll)

BUCKETS

30 piece Shrimp Bucket	31.99
6 piece Cod	12.99
6 piece Jack Salmon	14.99
6 piece Catfish	16.99

SANDWICHES

Porter Burger	2.99
Chicken Breast Sandwich	3.69
Cod Sandwich	3.59
Catfish Sandwich	4.79

(With Cheese - Add .40)

SIDES

Mushrooms	2.99
Toasted Ravioli (12 pcs.)	3.99
Corn Fritters (10 pcs.)	3.49
Jalapeno Poppers	4.59
French Fries	1.89
Onion Rings	2.39
Okra	3.49
Rolls	.40 each / 2.59 dozen
Jalapeno Peppers	.40
Ind. Slaw / Mashed Potatoes	1.39
Cheesecakes	1.99 & 5.99
Pies	2.69
Individual Chicken Pieces	

(Leg 1.39) (Thigh 1.39) (Wing 1.29) (Breast 1.99)

DRINKS

Coffee, Tea, Soda	1.09	1.19	1.29

SALADS

	PINT	GALLON
Creamy Cole Slaw	2.99	15.99
Potato Salad	3.49	16.99
Mashed Potatoes, Gravy	2.99	15.99
Green Beans		13.99
Pork & Beans		13.99

See our Catering Menu on the back

Photo credit: Porters Fried Chicken

Chicken may rule the roost at Porter's but fish shares star status with the yard bird. Catfish, jacks, shrimp, and cod are fried daily and available by the piece or bucket.

LONDON'S WING HOUSE

When I'm craving fried chicken, especially wings (my favorite piece of the bird!), I head north for a box of wings from London's Wing House.

London's Wing House may have a familiar ring. It began as London & Son's, the creation of Hildred and Dale London, St. Louis's legendary restaurateurs who first established the wing house in 1963. It closed in 2006, but it didn't stay shuttered long. Like the mythical phoenix rising from the ashes, London's Wing House was reopened by the Londons's son Patrick in 2010 and has since grown, now numbering three northside locations. A winged victory for London's fans!

Wing dinners are sold as three- to five-piece dinners, with sides of either fries or rice and gravy. Toss in a dinner roll and the plate is complete. If wings aren't your favorite piece, then order legs, thighs, or breast fritters. Barnyard gourmands might opt for livers and/or gizzards. If you eat livers, these are among the best—breaded and fried up the same as the wings. No matter the chicken plate you pick, when the cashier asks if you want that with hot sauce and ketchup, say yes. That's the famous London touch, finished with a generous zig-zag squirt of their hot sauce–ketchup combo over the top of the plate.

6209 Dr. Martin Luther King Dr., St. Louis
314-385-3131
londonswinghouse.com

Photo credit: London's Wing House

HODAK'S RESTAURANT & BAR

Fried chicken is more than a craving for some folks. It's a religion, so to speak. Devotees will travel almost anywhere from roadside stands to fancy restaurants to sample the latest version of the barnyard bird. However, the best birds are almost always found in your own hometown at neighborhood eateries and drive-throughs. Places you grew up with. Places with a personal history, where birthdays were celebrated and bags of take-home dinners were a special treat. Places like Hodak's, southside St. Louis's venerated house of hen.

Hodak's began as a humble place that changed locations over the years before landing at the corner of Gravois and McNair Avenues, where it has grown, taking up half the block to accommodate its ever-growing legions of faithful fans. Said fans will gladly wait for tables in lines that snake through the dining rooms and out the door before spilling onto the sidewalk.

The line moves fairly fast, and the time moves faster when downing a beer or counting chickens, that is, the assorted artsy chickens that decorate the place. I count the trays of fried chicken leaving the kitchen, which stokes my appetite and encourages me to hold steady in line.

2100 Gravois Ave., St. Louis
314-776-7292
hodaks.com

Photo credit: Suzanne Corbett

Generations of St. Louisans have come to Hodak's to celebrate their birthday where they've been treated to a free chicken dinner. It's not free anymore, but it is half-price, and that's something to celebrate.

Mexican cooks love chicken—chicken tamales, chicken enchiladas, chicken tacos and quesadillas. And let's not forget Amigo Joe's southern-style fried chicken. Perhaps I should say south-of-the-border fried chicken. It's a spicy, crispy chicken that Joe, the head amigo, decided to add to the menu after buying a pressure fryer at an auction, an impulse purchase that led Joe on a three-year quest to develop just the right marinade and breading for his chicken. He refined the recipe while getting feedback from the customers to whom he fed free samples. The end result was a habanero chili marinade, which in spite of the habanero's flame-throwing reputation, delivers a surprisingly subtle, spicy heat that lands somewhere in the middle of slightly spicy to killer inferno hot. For the chili-sensitive, Joe's has a regular version without the heat.

When chicken hit Amigo Joe's menu, it was segregated—off the main menu and out of the main dining room. Amigo Joe's fried chicken had its own exclusive dining room and entrance, which was always busy. It didn't take long to discover that chicken was an asset that gave customers a pleasant option, especially for those wanting something other than Mexican food. That's when the dining room segregation ended and chicken was added to the menu. It proved a win for all. Customers got chicken on the menu and Amigo Joe's got an expanded bar in the once-chicken-only dining room.

5901 Southwest Ave., St. Louis
314-645-1995
amigojoesstl.com

Photo credit: (left) Jim Corbett III; (right, both) Amigo Joe's

Skip the traditional sides. Take that plate a little farther south of the border with sides of beans and rice.

THE PICCADILLY
AT MANHATTAN

Turn-of-the-century, two-story, storefront houses have a comforting effect on a neighborhood. Such is the case of the Maplewood eatery The Piccadilly at Manhattan, a fixture of the neighborhood since 1901. Named for its address at the intersection of Piccadilly and Manhattan, it seems more like a place where grandma would have lived than a busy restaurant. That said, I wouldn't be surprised if there wasn't a grandma overseeing the kitchen where Piccadilly's signature comfort chicken is cooked. Crispy fried half-chickens and creamy chicken pot pies fly out of the kitchen year-round.

These two chicken recipes may well link Piccadilly's to its past. That's not a stretch considering that The Piccadilly at Manhattan has been a gathering place since its beginning and is now operated by the third, fourth, and fifth generations of the original owners, the Collidas.

Nonetheless, Piccadilly loves its chicken duo. Its fried chicken makes its fair share of "best of" lists. The chicken pot pie comes with a creamy chicken- and veggie-laced filling and is dished and topped with a blanket of puff pastry. The pot pie has been proclaimed a masterpiece by food critics, and most importantly by Piccadilly's customers; kudos that have raised the dish to cover-girl status when it was featured on *Sauce Magazine*'s November 2011 cover touting comfort food to be thankful for.

7201 Piccadilly Ave., St. Louis
314-646-0016
thepiccadilly.com

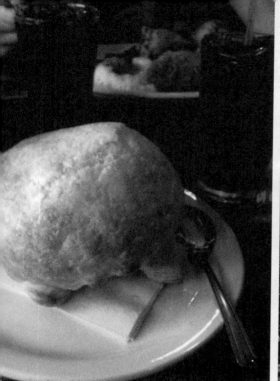

Photo credit: The Piccadilly at Manhattan

Cozy down and get comfortable on Piccadilly's patio while the weather allows. The pleasant surroundings enhance the flavor of the Chicken Pot Pie–or for that matter anything else ordered off the menu.

There's a lot to be said for Gallagher's, the eastside restaurant that has scored consistent titles as St. Louis's best fried chicken. Yes, even though Gallagher's is located in downtown Waterloo, thirty minutes from the Jefferson Barracks Bridge, it has snatched the coveted honor numerous times from a flock of worthy competitors.

What makes Gallagher's fried chicken an award winner is debatable. Some say it's the recipe and the way it's fried. I think it has a lot to do with terroir, or the environment, culture, and history that contribute to taste. I know that sounds highfalutin, but I swear it's true. There's something about riding through the Illinois farmland and settling down to a platter of chicken served in a historic building off an old town square that just makes it taste better. That's terroir at its best and what all those Sunday drives to find a country dinner were all about. Gallagher's country dinners are served family style—chicken is the center of the plate, and it's served with real mashed potatoes and pan gravy. Dinners are worth the drive and the wait, even if the line is out the door. It's part of the experience at Gallagher's.

114 W Mill St., Waterloo, IL
618-939-9933
gallagherswaterloo.com

Photo credit: Gallagher's

DINERS, DELIS, AND DRIVE-IN DIVES

THE HAVEN

The Haven, where burgers have been flipped for more than sixty years. The Haven is the ultimate corner tavern, where the daily blue plate special and beer are as good as it gets.

6625 Morganford Rd., St. Louis
314-352-4283, thehavenpub.com

Photo credit: The Haven

Since 1959 there haven't been a lot of changes at Carl's Drive Inn. The last change was big enough. That's when Carl's was transformed from a gas station into a hamburger shack, a changeup that's kept this relic of the old Route 66 thriving as a venerated burger stand, surviving through decades of change and fast-food burger wars. Carl's was never concerned with burger wars—they knew their success was their loyal customers who appreciated flattop-grilled, spatula-smashed burgers, fries, and frosty mugs of barrel-dispensed root beer. The menu is limited to burgers and fries with shakes, chili, tamales, and what could be considered Carl's gourmet item, the Curly-Q hot dog.

Like the menu, the building is small. Two countertops corral the workers between fryers, the grill, and soda taps. Each counter is lined with eight swivel stools. Nabbing a seat is luck of the draw. Sometimes you get lucky and get a seat, sometimes not. Just crowd in with the rest and stand shoulder to shoulder and shout out that order to go.

9033 Manchester Rd., St. Louis
314-961-9652
facebook.com/pages/Carls-Drive-Inn/111539875550923

Don't let the crowd scare you away. Park, get out, and wait. Your order will be taken soon.

ROOT BEER 1.50/2.50
FLOATS 3.00/5.00
SHAKES 3.00 5.00
SODAS 1.50/2.50
HOT TEA/COCOA 1.00
COFFEE 1.50

+ NEW ++
DREWES CONCRETE * 3.00
E, VANILLA, STRAWBERRY +
E'S ROCKY MOUNTAIN 4.00

FOOT LONG HOT DOG 3.25
FOOT LONG CHILI DOG 4.25
CURLY-O-HOT DOG 3.00
HAMBURGER 3.25
DOUBLE
TRIPLE 4.25
CHEESE BURGER 3.50
DOUBLE 3.25
TRIPLE 4.75
GRILLED CHEESE 6.25
FISH FILLET 3.00
CHICKEN FILLET 4.50

FRITO PIE 4.00
CHILI-3-WAYS 5.00
TAMALE & SAUCE 3.25
TAMALE & CHILI 3.25
CHILI
FRENCH FRIES 1.50/2.25
ONION RINGS 1.75
JALAPENOS
LETTUCE & TOMATO
GRILLED ONIONS
CHEESE SAUCE
BACON

Photo credit: Suzanne Corbett

WHITE KNIGHT DINER

Among St. Louis's most storied diners and drive-ins, the White Knight Diner has celebrity status—not so much for its tiny 600-square-foot, six-stool greasy-spoon looks, or its no-frills diner fare, which I find best enjoyed on an empty stomach or when the munchies hit. These are all excellent credentials that attracted attention from the Travel Channel and Food Network, but what gave the White Knight its fame was Universal Pictures choosing it as the location for its 1990 film White Palace.

During shooting, the diner got a facelift, not to mention a name change, switching after filming to White Knight. It had been the Super Sandwich Shop back in the day, when I ate my share of late-night cheeseburgers and diners enjoyed its unique clientele. It was an experience that still can be had, just not at night. Downtown is different now, so the White Knight serves breakfast and lunch, closing at 3 p.m. (2 p.m. on Saturdays). As for the menu, it's pretty much the same. Early birds often order breakfasts of hot cakes and slingers. Noontime rush will witness lunch plates of burgers, chili dogs, and triple-decker turkey clubs passed along the counter. They're all cooked the way you want and priced the way a diner should be—cheap.

1801 Olive St., St. Louis
314-621-5949
facebook.com/whiteknightdiner

Photo credit: White Knight Diner

Every city has its culinary landmarks, places revered for generations, representing local culture while defining the community through foods that never wane in popularity. Case in point, Gioia's and its hot salami sandwich—the only St. Louis winner of the James Beard Foundation America's Classics Award, which honors regional culinary treasures.

Gioia's opened on The Hill in 1918 as a grocery that made the family's homemade salam de testa (hot salami) in a building made of brick and wood repurposed from the 1904 St. Louis World's Fair. Cathy Donley bought Gioia's in 1980. She flipped it from a grocery into a sandwich shop, keeping hot salami as its signature. Cathy now works with her son Alex, who helped take Gioia's off The Hill in 2014 via a food truck, a winning business move that co-owner Alex opened as a default when he couldn't get a loan for another location but could get a loan for a car, aka the food truck. Soon after Gioia's food truck hit the street, it opened its second brick and mortar location downtown on Pine Street, feeding St. Louis's weekday lunch crowd.

At this point you may ask, what the hell is hot salami? Hot salami is a simple sausage, mildly spiced and boiled. It's sliced while it's still hot, explaining its name. Hot salami is stacked high on your bread choice and dressed the way you want. I take my hot salami with pepper cheese and giardiniera on garlic bread. Those out there who aren't hot salami fans need not worry. Remember, Gioia's is a deli. There are lots of choices.

1934 Macklind Ave., St. Louis
314-776-9410
gioiasdeli.com

Photo credit: (top left, bottom row) Gioia's Deli; (top right) Suzanne Corbett

Porknado, The Hogfather, and the Spicy Daggett:
Sandwiches that take Hot Salami to the next level.

BONES FRENCH QUARTER BAR & GRILL

"Never judge a book by its cover" is a rule that applies to Bones French Quarter. A plain and no-frills kind of place set off Manchester Road, it frankly isn't the prettiest building in Ballwin. And its name doesn't seem to fit the location. Reason enough to stop for a beer, check the menu, and get its story, a story that spans nearly 60 years and revolves around a sandwich, the Beef and Brick.

True to its name, Bones French Quarter has Cajun food—lots of it—including mountains of crawfish and plenty of gator. All good, but it can't compete with the Beef and Brick, the creation of Ray "Bones" Probst, who took the place over in 1989. To make a Beef and Brick, you first take thinly sliced moist roast beef, then top it with melted brick cheese and double stack it on toasted egg bread or Texas toast. It's one of those sandwiches that requires mastering the correct squishing technique to get it inside your mouth without having it fall apart in your hands.

Of course, po'boys and burgers are easier to handle, but they're not the same. When you're craving a Beef and Brick, nothing else will do. It's a one-of-a-kind West County special you won't find elsewhere. It has been a favorite for generations; some even consider being old enough to order your own Beef and Brick with a beer a rite of passage.

14766 Manchester Rd., Ballwin
636-391-8293
fqstl.com

Photo credit: (left and bottom right) Suzanne Corbett; (top right) Bones French Quarter Bar & Grill

West County's best kept secret for breakfast, until now. The house breakfast special: Punks one-pound Breakfast Burrito.

SPENCER'S GRILL

Time is a big thing at Spencer's Grill. For starters, check Spencer's operating hours: 6 a.m. to 2 p.m.—so eat up during breakfast and lunch because if you're hungry for supper or late-night burgers, you're out of luck.

Spencer's also seems like it's stuck in a time warp. It's like a 1950-ish time capsule: Formica counters and tabletops and red vinyl chrome stools. Trust me, this stuff is eye candy for mid-century modern enthusiasts. Finally, there's the neon sign hung outside over the front window, a sign that dates the place to 1947. This sign is a virtual work of art, complete with a clock—thought to be the only working clock on a neon sign west of the Mississippi.

With all this talk, it's about time to check out Spencer's menu. It hasn't any time restrictions. Order anything you want from the menu any time. Want French toast before closing or cheeseburgers when the doors open? Sure. Regulars recommend the sausages dipped in pancake batter that are fried and topped with sausage gravy for breakfast or the cheesesteak for lunch. Another staple is pie, sold by the slice. Just remember the time and try to avoid the morning and noon rushes. Otherwise, you'll have to spend a little time waiting.

223 S Kirkwood Rd., St. Louis
314-821-2601
facebook.com/pg/spencersgrill

Photo credit: Suzanne Corbett

GOODY GOODY DINER

Good food at a good location is a good thing. Just ask anyone who eats at Goody Goody Diner, which has operated at its same Natural Bridge address for nearly 70 years. It's an impressive location steeped in food history, beginning with Goody Goody, which sits on the site of St. Louis's first A&W Root Beer. The building would later be incorporated into Goody Goody's first building. Next door was Melrose Pizzeria, and down the street was Ed's White Front BBQ and Sam the Watermelon Man. Ted Drewes even got his start here, opening his first St. Louis operation six hundred yards east. All gone, except for Goody Goody.

Goody Goody's staying power is credited to community support and a comfort-filled menu as varied as a smorgasbord. Many come for the chicken and waffles served plain or drizzled with a spicy honey glaze—an add-on for fifty cents. Or fill up on meatloaf, an omelet, or the 1950s BBQ slaw burger.

At Goody Goody, the crowds can get thick. Just chill out and wait—tables turn over fast. Wait time is a great time to interact and enjoy Goody Goody's host, Sylvester Bell, who greets all with a smile and a personalized, impromptu poem to brighten your day.

5900 Natural Bridge Ave., St. Louis
314-383-3333
goodygoodydiner.com

Photo credit: Goody Goody Diner

It's all good.

PROTZEL'S DELICATESSEN

When New Yorkers report liking your corned beef better than any corned beef in New York, take notice. That's impressive kudos for corned beef, but Protzel's proves corned beef isn't just another pretty meat in the case. The difference is that Protzel's uses a family recipe that creates a custom-cured meat that is then sliced and served. The quintessential Jewish deli meat is best served simply—sliced and stacked on Jewish rye and smeared with spicy mustard. It's a classic.

Beyond the corned beef, Protzel's roasts its own turkey and makes its own pastrami, another rarity in today's deli trade. It's an Old World approach—making as much as they possibly can in house—that makes this deli fun. So bring your appetite and shop the cases. Consider the homemade knishes, kugels, chopped liver, or Joanie's chicken soup with matzo balls. Adventurous gourmands will want to try the kishke. I call it the Jewish answer to haggis. Or perhaps you'd like to try something more mainstream, like a Reuben. If you're a traditionalist, order the classic Reuben. For hipsters, try the Rachel, aka a turkey Reuben. If you're an indecisive connoisseur, go for the corned beef and pastrami Reuben, with a knish and a pickle on the side.

7608 Wydown Blvd., Clayton
314-721-4445
protzelsdeli.com

Photo credit: Protzel's Delicatessen

CHILI MAC'S DINER

The St. Louis World's Fair in 1904 was food paradise. Foods emerged from the fair that forever changed how and what we eat. My favorite food from the World's Fair isn't the ice cream cone or the hot dog. It's chili, the chili served at O.T. Hodge Chili Parlor. It's the same recipe that's served at Chili Mac's, the last of the downtown chili parlors. Chili Mac's calls itself a diner, but John Dirten, O.T. Hodge's nephew who ran a number of the Big Ed's Chili Mac's before retiring, always defined Chili Mac's as a chili parlor that served food.

True enough. There's diner food, burgers, scrambled eggs, and such. But if you go to Chili Mac's, have the chili or at least order something covered in chili, like a chilidog.

If you've never had O.T. Hodge's chili, which is actually the Edmond's brand made in south St. Louis, it has a taste like no other, a flavor rich in cumin with an almost creamy texture made without beans, but beans are optional and added on request. Chili Mac's chili at its best is served as a solitary bowl with crackers. After you have that, go crazy. Try the tamales wet (with chili) or have it ladled over spaghetti. Otherwise, get the Slinger.

510 Pine St., St. Louis
314-412-9040
facebook.com/chili-macs-diner-242014260619

Photo credit: (left, right center) Suzanne Corbett; (top right, bottom), Chili Mac's Diner

Legendary St. Louis-style chili served anyway you want it, with or without beans.

ILLINOIS

ALTON

Fast Eddie's Bon Air
1530 E 4th St.

BELLEVILLE

Eckert's Country Store & Farms
951 S Green Mount Rd.

BREESE

Ski Soda & Excel Bottling
488 S Broadway

FAIRMONT CITY

Tienda El Ranchito Mexican Restaurant & Grocery Store
2565 N 32nd St.

GRAFTON

Fin Inn
1500 W Main St.
Great River Rd. (Route 100)

HIGHLAND

Diamond Mineral Springs
1 W Pocahontas Rd.

WATERLOO

Gallagher's
114 W Mill St.

MISSOURI

BALLWIN

Bones French Quarter Bar & Grill
14766 Manchester Rd.

St. Louis Home Fires
15053 Manchester Rd.

CLAYTON

Protzel's Delicatessen
7608 Wydown Blvd.

CHESTERFIELD

Balaban's
1772 Clarkston Rd.

The Smokehouse Market
16806 Chesterfield Airport Rd.

Viviano's
150 Four Seasons Plaza

CLARKSVILLE

Overlook Farm
901 South Highway 79

COTTLEVILLE

Stone Soup Cottage
5809 Highway N

ELLLISVILLE

Massa's Of Course!
15310 Manchester Rd.

EUREKA

Sarah's Cake Shop on Central
127 S Central Ave.

FENTON

Pick-A-Bone
2599 Highway 141

Stuckmeyer's Farm Market and Greenhouse
249 Schneider Dr.

Viviano's
62 Fenton Plaza

FERGUSON

Paul's Market
1020 N Elizabeth Ave.

KIMMSWICK

The Blue Owl Restaurant and Bakery
6116 Second St.

MARYLAND HEIGHTS

Thies Farm and Greenhouses
14101 Creve Coeur Mill Rd.

ROCK HILL

Charcoal House
9855 Manchester Rd.

ST. ALBANS

The Old Barn Inn and Head's Store at The Inns of St. Albans
3516 St. Albans Rd.

ST. CHARLES

Asia at Ameristar Casino Resort Spa St. Charles
1 Ameristar Blvd.

ST. PETERS

Erio's Ristorante
951 Jungermann Rd.

ST. LOUIS

Adriana's on The Hill
5101 Shaw Ave.

Al-Tarboush Deli
602 Westgate Ave.

Al's Restaurant
1200 North First St.

Amighetti's Bakery & Cafe
5141 Wilson Ave.

Amigo Joe's
5901 Southwest Ave.

Anheuser-Busch
1200 Lynch St.

Assumption Greek Orthodox Church's Friday Greek Lunch
1755 Des Peres Rd.

Bevo Mill
4749 Gravois Ave.

Bixby's
Missouri History Museum
5700 Lindell Blvd.

Boathouse
6101 Government Dr.

Café Madeleine at the Piper Palm House
Tower Grove Park
4256 Magnolia Ave.

Café Osage
4605 Olive St.

Café Telegraph
2650 Telegraph Rd.

Carl's Drive Inn
9033 Manchester Rd.

Charlie Gitto's Downtown
207 N Sixth St.

Chili Mac's Diner
510 Pine St.

Cielo
999 N Second St.

Clementine's Naughty and Nice Creamery
1637 S 18th St.

Crown Candy Kitchen
1401 St. Louis Ave.

Dalie's Smokehouse
2951 Dougherty Ferry Rd.

DiGregorio's Market
5200 Daggett Ave.

Dressel's Public House
419 N Euclid Ave.

El Chico Bakery
2634 Cherokee St.

Feasting Fox
4200 S Grand Blvd.

Federhofer's Bakery
9005 Gravois Rd.

G & W Sausage Company
4828 Parker Ave.

Gelato Di Riso
5204 Wilson Ave.

Gioia's Deli
1934 Macklind Ave.

Goody Goody Diner
5900 Natural Bridge Ave.

Grbic
4071 Keokuk St.

Hodak's Restaurant & Bar
2100 Gravois Ave.

Ices Plain & Fancy
2256 S 39th St.

India Palace
11380 Natural Bridge Rd.

Jay International Foods
3172 S Grand Blvd.

John D. McGurk's
1200 Russell Blvd.

Kemoll's
One Metropolitan Square
211 N Broadway

Lemmon's by Grbic
5800 Gravois Ave.

Lona's Lil Eats
2199 California Ave.

London's Wing House
6209 Dr. Martin Luther King Dr.

LoRusso's Cucina
3121 Watson Rd.

Milagro Modern Mexican
20 Allen Ave. #130

Panorama
Saint Louis Art Museum, Forest Park
1 Fine Arts Dr.

Pappy's Smokehouse
3106 Olive St.

Pho Grand
3195 South Grand Blvd.

Piccione Pastry
6197 Delmar Blvd.

Piekutowski's European Style Sausage
4100 N Florissant Ave.

Planter's House
1000 Mississippi Ave.

Porter's Fried Chicken
3628 South Big Bend Rd.

Rigazzi's
4945 Daggett Ave.

Soulard Farmers Market
730 Carroll St.

Southern
3108 Olive St.

Spencer's Grill
223 S Kirkwood Rd.

Square One Brewery and Distillery
1727 Park Ave.

St. Raymond's Maronite Cathedral's Cedars Banquet Hall
Wednesday Lebanese Lunch
931 Lebanon Dr.

Sugarfire Smoke House
9200 Olive Blvd.

Sump Coffee
3700 S Jefferson Ave.

The Fountain on Locust
3037 Locust St.

The Haven
6625 Morganford Rd.

The Lemp Mansion Restaurant & Inn
3322 DeMenil Pl.

The Missouri Baking Company
2027 Edwards St.

The Piccadilly at Manhattan
7201 Piccadilly Ave.

The Scottish Arms
8 S Sarah Ave.

The Tenderloin Room
232 N Kingshighway Blvd.

Three Sixty
Hilton St. Louis at the Ballpark
1 S Broadway

Tiny Bar
1008 Locust Ave.

Tony's
410 Market St.

Urban Chestnut Brewing Company
URB (Urban Research Brewery)
4501 Manchester Ave.

UC Grove Brewery & Bierhall
4465 Manchester Ave.

Volpi Foods
5258 Daggett Ave.

White Knight Diner
1801 Olive St.

STE. GENEVIEVE

The Grapevine Grill at Chaumette
24345 State Route WW

VALLEY PARK

Fritz's Frozen Custard (West County)
815 Meramec Station Rd.

WEBSTER GROVES

Robust
227 W Lockwood Ave.

WILDWOOD

Big Chief
17352 Manchester Rd.

WRIGHT CITY

Cedar Lake Cellars
11008 Schreckengast Rd.

APPENDIX

PLATES WITH VIEWS AND GARDENS

DESTINATION DINING

GLASSES AND MUGS